# Grounded for life

## The Contractor's Survival Guide to Electrical Safety

Bobby Duncan

CESCP | NCCER Electrical Instructor | WSO-CSI Master Trainer

OSHA-Authorized Outreach Trainer (Construction)

U.S. Army Electrician (15 years) | U.S. Navy Seabee Electrician

Standards, Discipline, and Survival — A Comprehensive Guide to Electrical Safety for Contractors and Institutions.

## Preface

### The Mental and Physiological Toll of Electrical Work

When most people think of electrical work, they picture sparks, arc flashes, and the obvious physical dangers. What often goes unspoken is the toll this trade takes on the mind and the body. It's not just about burns and shocks, it's about the invisible weight carried long after the tools are put down.

### The Mental Toll

#### Hyper-Awareness

Electrical work requires constant focus. There's no room for autopilot. One wandering thought can mean disaster. Over time, that level of vigilance rewires your brain, leaving you anxious, restless, and unable to switch off—even at home.

Responsibility

Every time you sign off on a permit, energize equipment, or say "it's safe," you're carrying the lives of your crew in your hands. That responsibility is heavy, and when something goes wrong, even if it wasn't your fault, you replay it in your head for years.

Trauma and Close Calls

Burns, explosions, and fatalities are realities in this trade. Some of us have stood over a coworker who didn't make it. Others have felt the heat of an arc blast inches away. These experiences leave scars that don't show on the skin but never fade from memory.

The Physiological Toll

Fatigue

Long shifts, overnight outages, and relentless schedules destroy your natural rhythm. Chronic fatigue dulls judgment and reaction times, making mistakes more likely—and mistakes in this field can be deadly.

Wear and Tear

Crawling through attics, hauling cables, getting in and out of gear—the trade punishes your back, knees, shoulders, and wrists. Add heavy PPE in extreme conditions, and the body breaks down fast.

Stress Chemistry

Living in constant "alert mode" floods your body with cortisol and adrenaline. Over time, it damages the immune system, raises blood pressure, and increases the risk of heart disease. This isn't just stress, it's a slow biological grind that shortens careers and lives.

Breaking the Silence: The Importance of Talking

The biggest danger in this industry isn't just the hazards we face, it's the silence we keep. Too many electricians bury what they've seen, the stress they carry, and the pain their bodies are screaming with. We tell ourselves to tough it out. We don't want to be the ones who look weak.

But silence kills.

Talking about the toll—whether it's with a coworker, a supervisor, or even at home—breaks the cycle. When we open up, we make it acceptable for others to do the same. That conversation might stop someone from burning out, walking off the job, or worse.

Just like we test our meters before trusting a circuit, we need to "test" our own mental health. Conversations are a form of PPE for the mind. They protect us from carrying too much alone. They remind us of we're not isolated in the struggle.

It doesn't have to be formal. Sometimes it's as simple as asking a buddy, "How are you holding up?" or telling a younger apprentice, "I've been there too." These talks build culture, and culture is what saves lives as much as lockout/tagout or an arc flash suit.

The Bigger Picture

The real danger comes when these tolls overlap. Exhaustion fuels stress. Stress makes injuries feel worse. Trauma drives insomnia, which adds more fatigue. It's a cycle that ages electricians' years ahead of their time.

Acknowledging this reality isn't weakness—it's survival. Electrical safety is about more than PPE and lockout/tagout. It's about protecting the whole worker: the body, the mind, and the life outside the jobsite. And that starts with breaking the silence and having the courage to talk.

Preface

This survival guide was written from the ground up, forged in the field and sharpened in the classroom. It speaks in the voice of a tradesman, a trainer, and a leader who has lived these lessons. These chapters are not theories; they are survival frameworks, born of experience and reinforced by standards. Every story, every case, and every control exist for one reason: so that you and your crew make it home. This is not a textbook. It is a survival guide for contractors, electricians, and leaders who refuse to leave safety to chance.

# Table of contents

Chapter 1 Mindset and Survival in Electrical Contracting

Chapter 2 Building a Safety First Electrical Culture

Chapter 3 Human Performance Error Prevention

Chapter 4 Electrical Safety Program

Chapter 5 Training, Certification

Chapter 6 Hazard recognition Risk assessment

Chapter 7 PPE Last line of defense

Chapter 8 LOTO

Chapter 9 Continuous improvement auditing

Chapter 10 Incident investigation Lessons learned

Chapter 11 Job Briefings & Pre-Task Planning

Chapter 12 Leadership Under Voltage: Your Survival Standard

Chapter 13 Cost of Complacency

Chapter 14 Inside the flash

Chapter 15 The call nobody wants to make

Chapter 16 Carrying Ghosts

Chapter 17 Survival Isn't an Accident — It's a Legacy

References

# Chapter 1

## Mindset and Survival in Electrical Contracting

"Genius is one percent inspiration and ninety-nine percent perspiration."
— Thomas A. Edison

# Chapter 1

Mindset is unseen PPE. Before a hood flips down or a glove seal at the wrist, the first protection a worker brings to work is the way they think. In this trade, the difference between a close call and a catastrophe is often measured in one decision: verify or assume, pause or push, speak up or stay quiet. Survival starts long before the first tool turns it starts with the honest belief that physics does not negotiate and that no deadline is worth a funeral.

The core rule I teach is simple: we don't trade life for minutes. Production pressure is real schedules slide, weather closes in, a critical path gets crowded, but pressure is not permission to cut steps. The disciplined mindset treats pressure as a variable to manage, not a reason to gamble. That is why we institutionalize practices like pre-job briefs, peer checks, and test-before-touch. These aren't bureaucratic boxes; they are speed multipliers. A crew that plans clearly and verifies honestly moves faster over time than a crew that sprints blind and trips over its own shortcuts.

A grounded mindset is built on two habits: humility and verification. Humility accepts that even veterans make mistakes. Verification refuses to let habit become proof. If a conductor might be energized, we treat it as energized until we have objective evidence otherwise. That means establishing an electrically safe work condition in line with recognized practice identifying the source, open the disconnecting means, apply lockout/tagout, verify absence of voltage with a properly rated tester that we prove on a known source before and after use (OSHA 1910.333; NFPA 70E 2024, Articles 110 and 120).

Mindset shows up in small choices long before it shows up in big events. An experienced hand sees an old tag and "knows" the feeder is still open. A grounded hand slows down. He reads the permit, touches his lock, checks the one-line, reviews the sequence, proves the meter, and only then breaks plane. One extra minute now prevents months of recovery. Discipline is not drama it's quietly doing the right thing when nobody is watching.

Fatigue and distraction undermine mindset like corrosion weakens copper: slowly, invisibly, then all at once. We treat them like hazards because they are hazards. If a worker shows the signs rushing, skipping verbal checks, re-reading labels, missing simple steps—we don't shame them. We slow down the job, rotate tasks, or stop and reset. Leaders model this by stopping themselves when they sense it. One authentic stop teaches more than a hundred slogans.

Another pillar of survival is psychological safety the trust that anyone can call a timeout and not be punished. "Stop Work Authority" is only real if it is used without retaliation. I make it visible: when a hand stops the work, the leader thanks them, we step back, and we re-brief. Ten minutes of regrouping beats ten months of physical therapy. Crews copy what leaders celebrate; if you celebrate silence, you will get silence.

Standards exist for a reason, and they are on our side. NFPA 70E makes hazard elimination the first priority. If we can de-energize, we do. If we cannot because of design, impracticality, or elevated risk we treat the task with strict controls: planning, justification, permits, and protection proportional to the hazard (NFPA 70E 2024, Article 110). OSHA requires employers to protect workers from electrical hazards and to control hazardous energy during servicing and maintenance (OSHA 1910.333; 1910.147). The mindset isn't "do we have to," it's "why wouldn't we."

Mindset also respects boundaries literally. Working clearances are not suggestions; they are lifelines. The National Electrical Code sets minimum space so a human can stand, move, egress, and recover without being pinned between live parts and hard edges (NEC 110.26). If material creeps in front of a gear door, the hazard isn't just a citation it's a blocked exit during a flash or a slip. A grounded crew protects that space like they protect their eyes.

Finally, mindset is teachable. We don't wait for good judgment to mysteriously arrive. We rehearse the job, talk through the "what-ifs," decide ahead of time what we'll do if the unexpected happens, and assign roles so nobody improvises alone. We build discipline touch your lock, say your verification out loud, hold the drawing in your hand when you point, re-state the isolation before contact, and confirm PPE is appropriate for the task. Repetition builds reflexes, and reflex saves lives when adrenaline tries to spend your attention for you.

I tell every crew I lead nobody gets paid enough to be a hero. We get paid to be professionals. Professionals make boring, safe choices again and again until a dangerous job looks ordinary. That's mindset. That's survival.

When I walk onto a job site, I don't just scan for hazards I listen for mindset. You can hear it in the way a journeyman talks to an apprentice, in the tone of a pre-job brief, in the silence before a panel is opened. A crew with the right mindset doesn't rush the quiet moments. They know that the most dangerous seconds are often the ones that feel routine. I've seen seasoned electricians skip steps because they've "done it a hundred times, and I've seen green hands save lives because they asked one honest question. That's why I teach mindset as a muscle it has to be exercised daily. You don't build it by surviving close calls; you build it by preventing them.

Mindset isn't just about what you do, it's about what you tolerate. If you let shortcuts slide, they become culture. If you ignore fatigue, it becomes normal. I've led crews through 100-degree heat, freezing rain, and midnight shutdowns, and I've learned that the strongest mindset is the one that respects the body. You can't think clearly when you're exhausted, dehydrated, or distracted. That's why I push hydration, rest cycles, and mental resets as hard as I push lockout/tagout. A clear head is part of your PPE.

I've always said that mindset is what shows up when the plan doesn't. You can have the best drawings, the cleanest scope, and the most detailed schedule—but when the unexpected hits, it's mindset that decides whether the crew adapts or panics. I've seen it play out in real time: a mislabeled breaker, a missing permit, a last-minute change from the GC. The crew that survive and thrive aren't the ones with the fanciest gear, they're the ones who stay calm, communicate clearly, and fall back on discipline.

Mindset also means knowing when to walk away. I've pulled crews off jobs that looked "almost ready" because the risk wasn't worth the reward. I've shut down energized work that had a permit but no justification. That's not easy. It takes backbone to say no when the pressures on. But that's what leadership is protecting your people even when it costs you comfort.

Mindset is also about how you respond to uncertainty. In electrical work, uncertainty isn't rare it's routine. You open a panel and find undocumented feeds, or you trace a circuit that doesn't match the one-line. That's when mindset separates the professional from the gambler. The professional doesn't guess. He steps back, calls for a second set of eyes, and treats the unknown like a live hazard until proven otherwise.

There's a myth in this trade that real electricians don't need to ask questions. That mindset gets people hurt. I've been in this game long enough to know that the smartest hands are the ones who speak up when something doesn't feel right. I've seen apprentices catch errors that veterans miss, simply because they were still curious. That's why I build crews where questions are welcomed, not punished.

Mindset also means knowing your limits. and respecting them. I've seen good hands get hurt because they didn't want to admit they were out of their depth. Pride is a silent hazard in this trade. It whispers, "You've got this," even when the situation calls for backup. That's why I teach my crew to speak plainly about what they know and what they don't. There's no shame in asking for help; the shame is in pretending you don't need it and putting others at risk.

I've worked with crews who had every certification in the book but still lacked the mindset to stay safe. Training gives you tools; mindset tells you when to use them. You can memorize NFPA 70E and still miss the moment when a peer needs a second check. You can pass a lockout/tagout test and still forget to verify voltage because you're distracted. That's why I say mindset is the glue that holds the training together.

Mindset is what keeps you honest when no one's watching. I've seen crews work flawlessly under supervision, only to cut corners the moment the lead walks away. That's not discipline that's performance. Real discipline is internal. It's a quiet decision to follow the process even when it's inconvenient, even when no one notices, even when you're tired and the shortcut looks tempting.

I've learned that mindset is contagious. One grounded hand can shift the tone of an entire crew. When someone takes the time to verify, to speak up, to slow down, it gives others permission to do the same. That's why I invest in my quiet leaders the ones who don't need a title to set the standard. Those habits ripple outward. And before long, you've got a crew that doesn't just follow safety they believe in it.

Mindset is what keeps the job human. We're not just managing hazards, we're managing people. I've seen how a single bad day can cloud judgment; how personal stress can bleed into professional decisions. That's why I check in with my crews beyond the task list. If someone's distracted, I don't just hand them a checklist, I ask what's going on. Because mindset isn't just technical it's emotional.

There's a difference between knowing the rules and believing in the mission. I've worked jobs where the safety manual was thick, laminated, and ignored. And I've worked with crews who had half the paperwork but twice the discipline. The difference was mindset. When people believe that safety is leadership, not liability, they act differently. They speak up. They slow down. They take pride in doing it right.

Mindset is what turns a crew into a unit. I've seen jobs where every person was technically skilled, but the team still failed because they didn't think together. Electrical work isn't just about individual performance it's about synchronized decisions. That's why I push team mindset just as hard as personal discipline. We brief together, we verify together, and we stop together.

I've watched mindset evolve over the years. When I started, safety was often treated like a box to check or a speech to endure. Now, I see more crews treating it like a craft—something to refine, practice, and take pride in. That shift didn't happen by accident. It happened because leaders started telling the truth: that survival isn't luck, it's discipline.

# Chapter 2

## Building a Safety-First Electrical Culture

"An investment in knowledge pays the best interest."
— Benjamin Franklin

## Chapter 2

Culture is safety's operating system. It runs quietly in the background of every project, deciding whether checklists get read or ignored, whether pre-job briefs are real conversations or recitations, whether a new apprentice feels free to say, "I don't understand." A written program can exist on paper, but a living culture exists in people. If the crew believes that production is the real measure and safety is theater, the program will fail in practice no matter how well it is written.

Culture starts with leadership modeling. Leaders are always teaching; the only question is what. When a foreman straps on arcrated gear without complaint, when a superintendent pauses a lift because a tag is unclear, when an owner asks, "What did we learn?" after a near miss instead of "Who do we blame?" people notice. Behavior at the top sets the altitude the crew will fly at.

Safety culture turns values into habits. We formalize the habits that keep us alive: real pre-job briefs, clear roles and responsibilities, hazard identification in plain language, and honest last-minute risk checks. We replace vague sayings like "be careful" with specific actions: identify the energy, isolate it, lock it, tag it, try it, and test for absence of voltage before we touch. We don't say "watch your hands"; we say, "both hands gloved before reaching into the cabinet."

Communication is the bloodstream of culture. We make it hard to misunderstand brief with drawings, touch the equipment while explaining, and ask each person to restate critical steps in their own words. We avoid sarcasm and shouting because fear shrinks attention. Calm direction under pressure is not a personality trait, it is a skill leaders practice.

Accountability in a healthy culture is not punishment; it's ownership. We hold the line on procedures because they are on the path home. When someone takes a shortcut, we correct the behavior and fix the conditions that made the shortcut attractive. We praise the stop more than the sprint. We investigate quietly and thoroughly, focusing on systems and signals, not rumor and ego.

Culture also depends on competence. Training is not a lecture, it's a series of small, repeatable reps until a task is automatic. We build competency through hands-on practice: tracing energy paths, writing lockout steps, selecting PPE appropriate to arc-flash hazards, and using meters correctly. We document training not to appease a regulator, but to track growth and identify gaps. The culture that learns stay safe because it stays curious.

Standards give culture a backbone. NFPA 70E requires employers to establish and document an electrical safety program and make hazard elimination the first priority. OSHA establishes the employer's duty to protect and to control hazardous energy during servicing and maintenance. The NEC defines installation and workspace conditions that make safe work possible. When culture and standards align, people stop arguing opinions and start following principles.

We also design culture for the worst day, not the best. We pre-plan emergencies, verify that access and egress are clear, stage first-aid equipment where it can be reached with gloved hands, and coordinate with site responders. A crew that has talked through "what if" responds like a team when it counts.

Finally, culture is a promise kept over time. It is a thousand small choices made the same way: we verify, we brief, we protect the work area, we respect the body's limits, we elevate concerns, and we thank the person who speaks up. The result is not only fewer injuries; it is better to work cleaner installs, fewer rework cycles, and clients who notice the difference.

Culture is built in the quiet moments when no one's watching, when the pressure's on, when the easy thing would be to look the other way. I've seen crews with all the right paperwork still miss the mark because the culture wasn't real. It was written but not lived. And I've seen small teams with minimal resources outperform bigger ones because they had something stronger than budget, they had belief.

Belief that safety wasn't a slogan. Belief that leadership meant protection. Belief that every person mattered.

I've walked into jobs where the tone was set before the first tool turned. You could feel it in the way the crew greeted each other, in the way the foreman asked questions instead of giving orders, in the way the apprentice was encouraged to speak up. That's culture. It's not a checklist, it's a climate. And it starts with how we treat people. If a worker feels disposable, they'll act disposable. But if they feel valued, they'll protect the job like it's their own name on the line.

Culture is also how we respond to mistakes. I've seen leaders blow up over a missed step, and I've seen leaders pull someone aside, ask what happened, and turn it into a teachable moment. The second approach builds trust. The first builds silence. And silence is deadly in this trade. If your crew is afraid to speak up, you've already lost. That's why I say to teams: we don't punish honesty we reward it. If you see something, say something. If you mess it up, own it. If you're unsure, ask. That's not weakness. That's strength.

A safety-first culture doesn't just protect bodies it protects minds. I've seen how stress, fatigue, and fear can cloud judgment. That's why we build in recovery time, rotate tasks, and check in with each other. If someone's off their game, we don't push we pause. Because culture isn't just about procedures it's about people. And people need care, not just compliance. I've seen more accidents caused by burnout than by bad wiring. That's why a real safety culture treats mental health as part of the job.

Culture also shows up in how we train. I don't believe in one-anddone training. I believe in repetition, reflection, and reinforcement.

We don't just teach the steps we teach the why. Why do we verify. Why do we lock it out? Why do we test before touch. When people understand the reason, they own the responsibility. And when they own it, they protect it. That's how you build a crew that doesn't just follow rules they live them.

I've seen culture shift when one person decides to lead. It doesn't take a title, it takes courage. I've watched apprentices ask hard questions and change the tone of a job. I've seen quiet hands stop a task and save a life. That's the power of culture—it multiplies. One good decision lead to another. One act of integrity sets a new standard. And before long, you've got a crew that doesn't just survive they thrive.

Culture is also about consistency. You can't preach safety on Monday and ignore it on Friday. You can't praise a stop one day and punish it the next. Crews remember what you celebrate. If you celebrate at speed, you'll get shortcuts. If you celebrate silence, you'll get silence. But if you celebrate discipline, verification, and courage you'll get a culture that lasts. That's why I make it a point to thank the person who speaks up, to highlight the crew that briefs well, to recognize the hand who double-checks. Those moments build the foundation.

We also build culture through design. If the layout of the jobsite makes safe work hard, we redesign it. If the schedule pressures people into rushing, we renegotiate it. If the PPE is uncomfortable or unavailable, we fix it. Culture isn't just attitude, it's infrastructure. You can't expect people to follow safety if the system fights them. That's why I work with planners, engineers, and owners to make sure the job supports the standard. Because culture isn't just what happens in the field, it's what's built into the blueprint.

A safety first culture is proactive, not reactive. We don't wait for the incident to prevent it. We walk through the job before it starts. We talk through the "what-ifs." We assign roles, rehearse responses, and verify readiness. That's not paranoia, it's preparation. And preparation is what separates the crews who survive from the ones who scramble. I've seen jobs go sideways and crews respond like clockwork not because they were lucky, but because they were ready.

Finally, culture is legacy. It's what you leave behind when the job is done. It's the reputation you build, the standard you set, the example you leave for the next generation. I've had apprentices tell me years later that one moment changed how they lead. One stop. One brief.

One correction. That's culture. It's not just about today, it's about tomorrow. And if we build it right, it outlasts us.

Culture is also how we handle transitions—new hires, new shifts, new scopes. I've seen strong crews lose their edge when a new face joins and no one takes the time to onboard them properly. That's not just a missed opportunity, it's a risk. A safety-first culture doesn't assume people know; it ensures they do. We walk the new hand through the site, explain the expectations, and pair them with someone who models the standard. We don't throw them into the deep end and hope they swim. We build trust from day one, because trust is the foundation of every safe decision that follows.

I've worked jobs where the culture was so strong, you could feel it in the air. People moved with purpose. They spoke with clarity. They looked out for each other. And when something didn't feel right, they stopped without hesitation. That kind of culture doesn't happen by accident, it's built through repetition, reinforcement, and leadership that refuses to compromise. It was built when the crew knew that safety isn't just a rule, it's a value. And values don't bend under pressure. They hold firm. That's what makes a culture resilient—not perfect conditions, but unwavering principles.

Culture also means knowing when to reset. I've led crews through shutdowns, outages, and high-pressure turnarounds, and I've learned that even the best teams need a moment to breathe. When the pace gets frantic, we pause. We regroup. We re-brief. Because fatigue doesn't ask permission it just shows up. And when it does, it erodes judgment, coordination, and attention. A safety-first culture doesn't push through blindly—it recalibrates. That's why I build in reset points. Not just for the job, but for the people doing it. Because a clear head is just as critical as a clear scope.

Culture is tested in the gray areas, the moments where the rules don't quite fit the situation, and judgment must step in. I've seen crews face unexpected conditions: mislabeled gear, undocumented feeds, last-minute scope changes. In those moments, culture decides whether the team pauses or pushes. A strong culture doesn't rely on perfect plans it relies on shared principles. We don't touch what we haven't verified. We don't assume safety, we prove it. That's why I teach crews to fall back on fundamentals when the job gets messy. Because when the plan breaks down, culture holds the line.

I've also seen culture break down when leadership gets quiet. When the foreman stops reinforcing the standard, when the superintendent starts tolerating shortcuts, when the owner shifts focus to speed over safety the crew follows. Culture is fragile. It doesn't erode all at once, it fades in small compromises. That's why I challenge leaders to stay loud about safety. Not just in meetings, but in the field. Not just after incidents, but before them. Because silence sends a message. And if that message is "safety is optional," the crew will hear it loud and clear.

Culture is built on clarity. If expectations are vague, enforcement becomes personal. And when enforcement feels personal, trust breaks. That's why I push for clear, written procedures that match the reality of the job. Not just what looks good on paper, but what works in the field. We involve the crew in writing them. We walk through them together. We adjust them when conditions change. Because when people help shape the standard, they're more likely to own it. And ownership is the difference between compliance and commitment.

Culture is also shaped by how we handle near misses. I've seen jobs where a close call was brushed off with a joke or buried under paperwork. That's a missed opportunity. A safety-first culture treats near misses like gold because they're warnings without the cost. We gather the crew, walk through what happened, and ask the hard questions: What signal did we miss? What assumption did we make? What system failed to catch it? We don't assign blame—we assign responsibility. Because every near miss is a second chance to get it right before someone gets hurt.

I've worked with crews who thought culture was just about attitude. But attitude without structure is just noise. A real safety culture has systems that support the mindset. That means clear escalation paths, documented stop-work protocols, and leadership that backs the crew when they use them. If a hand calls a timeout and gets punished, the culture is broken. But if that same hand gets thanked, briefed, and supported, the culture grows stronger. That's why I make it a point to reinforce the system every time it's used. Because culture isn't just what we say it's what we protect.

Culture also lives in the details. I've seen jobs where the PPE was technically compliant but practically useless gloves that didn't fit, face shields that fogged, gear that slowed the work so much it encouraged shortcuts. That's not safety that's sabotage. A safety-first culture listens to the crew. If the gear doesn't work, we fix it. If the process is clunky, we streamline it. Because the goal isn't just compliance—it's usability. When the tools support the task, the crew supports the standard. And that's how you build a culture that lasts beyond the audit.

Culture is reinforced by how we handle feedback. I've seen crews where suggestions were dismissed, and I've seen crews where feedback reshaped the job. The difference is humility. A safety-first culture doesn't pretend to have all the answers it listens. When a hand says, "This doesn't feel right," we don't argue we investigate. When someone suggests a better way to isolate, we test it. That's how culture evolves. Not through mandates, but through collaboration. Because the people closest to the hazard often have the clearest view of the solution.

I've led teams where culture was the only thing holding the job together. The schedule was tight, the scope was shifting, and the client was breathing down our necks. But the crew stayed grounded not because the conditions were ideal, but because the culture was strong. We briefed every morning, verified every step, and backed each other up. That's what culture does it stabilizes the job when everything else is unstable. It gives the crew something solid to stand on when the ground starts to shake.

Culture also means knowing when to say, "not yet." I've walked jobs where the gear was energized, the permit was incomplete, and the pressure was high. And I've told the client, "We're not ready." That's not defiance, it's discipline. A safety-first culture doesn't chase deadlines, it protects lives. We don't start until the conditions are right. That means the paperwork is clean, the isolation is verified, the PPE is appropriate, and the crew is briefed. Anything less is gambling. And in this trade, gambling gets people hurt.

Culture is shaped by how we handle conflict. I've seen crews fall apart not because of technical failure, but because of unresolved tension. A safety-first culture doesn't avoid conflict—it manages it. If two hands disagree on a step, we don't let ego decide—we let the process guide us. We go back to the drawing, the permit, the standard. We ask questions, not make accusations. Because when conflict is handled with respect and clarity, it strengthens the crew. It shows that safety isn't personal—it's procedural. And that mindset keeps the job focused and the team united.

I've worked with crews where culture was tested by outsiders— contractors who didn't share the same standards, vendors who cut corners, clients who pushed for speed. In those moments, the crew has a choice: bend to pressure or hold the line. A strong culture doesn't compromise when others do. It educates, it reinforces, and if needed, it escalates. I've had to walk vendors off a site because they refused to follow lockout protocols. That's not a dramatical discipline. Because culture isn't just internal, it's contagious. And if we don't protect it, it gets diluted.

Culture also shows up in how we close out a job. I've seen crews finish a project and leave behind chaos unlabeled gear, missing documentation, unsecured panels. That's not just sloppy, it's unsafe. A safety-first culture finishes strong. We verify every isolation, label, every feed, document every change. We walk the site as if the next crew's life depends on it—because it might. That's why I teach my teams to treat closeout like startups. With the same care, the same discipline, the same mindset. Because culture isn't just how we begin, it's how we end.

Leadership in a safety-first culture isn't about control—it's about clarity. I've seen foremen try to lead through authority alone, and it always backfires. The best leaders don't just give orders, they give context. They explain the why behind what. They connect the task to the risk, the risk to the standard, and the standard to the crew's survival. That kind of clarity builds trust. And trust is what turns a group of workers into a team. When people understand the mission, they protect it. That's leadership—not just directing the work but anchoring it in purpose.

I've learned that leadership means being the first to stop. When something feels off, when the plan starts to drift, when the crew gets quiet, I don't wait. I call the timeout. I model the pause. Because crews copy what leaders do, not what they say. If I rush, they'll rush. If I skip steps, they'll skip steps. But if I slow down, verify, and regroup, they'll follow. That's why I tell every leader I train: your habits are contagious. Make sure they're worth catching.

Leadership also means protecting the crew from invisible pressure. I've had owners push for faster turnover, clients demand last-minute changes, and schedulers compress timelines without understanding the risk. My job as a leader is to absorb that pressure and not pass it down. I shield the crew from unrealistic demands, advocate for safe pacing, and negotiate scope when needed. That's not weakness it's wisdom. Because the crew's safety is my responsibility, and no external pressure justifies internal compromise.

leadership means legacy. Every job we lead is a chance to leave something better behind—a stronger standard, a safer crew, a clearer process. I've had apprentices become foremen, foremen become trainers, and trainers become advocates—all because someone took the time to lead with integrity. That's the real reward. Not just a clean installation, but a culture that outlasts the job. Because when leadership is grounded in safety, the impact doesn't end at turnover it echoes through every crew that follows.

Culture is sustained by storytelling. I've seen how one powerful story a close call, a courageous stop, a lesson learned can ripple through a crew and reshape behavior. That's why I encourage leaders to share real experiences. Not just the polished wins, but the hard-earned lessons. When a foreman talks about the time, he missed a step and got lucky, it reminds the crew that luck isn't a strategy. When an apprentice shares how speaking up prevented a mistake, it reinforces that every voice matters. Stories stick. And when they're grounded in truth, they build a culture that remembers.

A safety-first culture also embraces evolution. What worked five years ago might not work today. New technologies, changing codes, and shifting jobsite dynamics require us to stay adaptable. I've seen crews cling to outdated habits because "that's how we've always done it. But culture isn't static, it's alive. We review, revise, and improve. We invite feedback, test new methods, and stay current with standards. That's how we stay sharp. Because the moment we stop evolving is the moment we start falling behind—and in this trade, falling behind can mean falling short of safety.

Culture thrives when it's celebrated. I make it a point to recognize the crews who do it right—not just with awards, but with respect. When a team consistently briefs well, verifies thoroughly, and supports each other, I let them know it's noticed. That kind of recognition reinforces the standard. It tells the crew that safety isn't just expected, it's appreciated. And appreciation fuels pride. When people take pride in their culture, they protect it. They pass it on.

They make it stronger. That's how a safety-first mindset becomes a legacy.

In the end, building a safety-first electrical culture is about choosing people over pressure, principles over shortcuts, and legacy over luck. It's about showing up every day with the mindset that every decision matters, every voice counts, and every life is worth protecting. I've seen what happens when culture is ignored—and I've seen what's possible when it's embraced. The difference is night and day. And for me, there's no question which side I want to be on. Because in this trade, culture isn't just how we work, it's how we live.

Chapter 3

Human Performance and Error Prevention

"To err is human, but to persevere in error is only the act of a fool."
— Cicero

# Chapter 3

Human error isn't a flaw, it's a fact. In electrical work, we don't get to pretend we're perfect. We must plan for the opposite. I've seen the sharpest hands make the simplest mistakes, not because they were careless, but because they were human. Fatigue, distraction, assumptions, pressure these aren't excuses, there are conditions. And if we don't design our systems to account for them, we're not building safety, we're building traps. That's why I teach crews to expect error, detect it early, and recover without harm. Because the goal isn't perfection—it's resilience.

I've worked jobs where the culture punished mistakes so harshly that people stopped reporting them. That's not safety, that's silence. And silence is dangerous. A safety-first culture doesn't hide error; it studies it. We ask, "What made this possible?" not "Who screwed up?" Because most incidents aren't caused by one bad decision, they're caused by a dozen small ones that went unchecked. That's why we build in checks, pauses, and peer reviews. Not because we don't trust our people but because we do. We trust them enough to give them systems that catch the slip before it becomes a scar.

Error prevention starts with honest conversations. I've seen foremen who bark orders and expect perfection, and I've seen foremen who ask questions and expect clarity. The second crew is safer every time. When people feel safe to speak up, they do. They ask, "Are we sure this is de-energized?" They say, "I'm not clear on this step." They admit, "I'm tired." That's not weakness it's wisdom. Because the most dangerous worker isn't the one who makes a mistake, it's the one who hides it. That's why we build crews where honesty is rewarded, and silence is corrected.

We also prevent errors by slowing down the moment before contact. I call it the "last quiet second." That's when the meter is in your hand, the panel is open, and the job is about to begin. If you rush at that moment, you risk everything. But if you pause, verify, and speak your steps out loud, you anchor your attention. I've seen this save lives. One journeyman paused, said "Line side verified," and the apprentice caught a mislabeled breaker. That's why I teach verbal verification—not just for clarity, but for safety. Because when adrenaline spikes, your voice can steady your hands.

I've seen error prevention fail because the system assumed people would always do the right thing. That's not realistic. People don't fail because they're reckless, they fail because they're rushed, distracted, or misinformed. That's why I teach crews to build friction into critical steps. We don't make it hard to do the job; we make it hard to skip safety. You shouldn't be able to energize without a permit. You shouldn't be able to remove a panel without verifying isolation. These aren't obstacles, they're safeguards. And when they're built into the workflow, they protect the crew from their own humanity.

One of the most powerful tools we have is the pre-job brief. But only if it's real. I've seen briefs that were just paperwork read fast, signed blind, forgotten by lunch. That's not a safety tool, that's a liability. A real brief is a conversation. We talk through the scope, the hazards, the sequence, and the roles. We ask questions. We challenge assumptions. We rehearse the unexpected. And we do it together. Because when the crew owns the plan, they protect it. And when they protect the plan, they protect each other.

Error prevention also means knowing your limits. I've seen good hands get hurt because they didn't want to admit they were out of their depth. Pride is a silent hazard in this trade. It whispers, "You've got this," even when the situation calls for backup. That's why I teach my crew to speak plainly about what they know and what they don't. There's no shame in asking for help; the shame is in pretending you don't need it and putting others at risk. A grounded mindset isn't about ego, it's about clarity. You know your role, your scope, your tools, and your boundaries. And when something falls outside that, you raise your hand.

Human performance isn't just about skill, it's about state. I've seen brilliant electricians make dangerous decisions because they were exhausted, distracted, or emotionally drained. That's why I show crews how to monitor each other not just for PPE, but for presence. If someone's zoning out, rushing, or repeating themselves, we pause. We checked in. We rotate tasks. Because error doesn't announce itself it creeps in. And if we wait for a mistake to prove it, we're already too late. A safety-first crew doesn't just watch the work they watch the worker.

We also design against error by simplifying complexity. I've seen procedures so convoluted that even experienced hands struggled to follow them. That's not safe, that's confusion. And confusion breeds mistakes. That's why I push for clarity in every step. We write lockout plans that make sense. We label gear in plain language. We use drawings that match the field. Because when the system is clear, the crew is confident. And confident crews don't guess they will verify.

Another key to prevention of error is redundancy. I've seen lives saved because someone double-checked a step that had already been verified. That's not overkill, it's discipline. We use peer checks, verbal confirmations, and sequence reviews not because we don't trust each other, but because we trust the process. And the process says: verify, then verify again. Because in this trade, one missed detail can change everything. Redundancy isn't a burden it's a backup plan for when the human brain gets tired.

I've seen how technology can help or hurt human performance. Smart meters, remote sensors, and digital permits can streamline the job. But if they're not understood, they become distractions. That's why I train crews to use tech as a tool, not a crutch. We verify readings manually. We test meters before and after use. We don't assume the screen is right, we prove it. Because no matter how advanced the gear gets, the human behind it still makes the call. And that call needs to be grounded in discipline.

Error prevention is also about recovery. I've seen crews freeze after a mistake, unsure what to do next. That's why we rehearse recovery just like we rehearse the job. If someone touches the wrong conductor, we know how to respond. If a step is missed, we know how to regroup. We don't panic we reset. Because the goal isn't to avoid every error to survive them. And survival comes from preparation, not perfection.

I have seen some Corporations use human performance tools like three-way communication and questioning attitude training. Workers repeat instructions, challenge unclear steps, and stop when unsure. These habits helped them maintain low incident rates. When culture protects the right to pause, people use it and they go home whole.

Some other corporations use a peer coaching model where experienced electricians mentor newer hands not just on skills, but on mindset. Coaches spot fatigue, distraction, and hesitation. They connect, not just correct. The result? Crews where psychological safety is real, and error is expected, caught, and corrected without shame.

But stories like these only matter if we translate them into daily discipline. Safety culture isn't built in classrooms or manuals, it's built on the job, in real time. It's in the foreman who calls for a pause before the lift. It's in the apprentice who speaks up about a mislabeled panel. It's in the journeyman who admits he's too tired to keep going. These are the moments that separate surviving from suffering.

The Human Element Expanded

When we talk about human performance, it's easy to reduce it to checklists, procedures, or "soft skills." But the truth is, human performance is the foundation of electrical safety. Every lockout tag, every arc-flash label, every PPE suits it all depends on the human being willing and able to use it correctly. And human beings don't walk onto the job as a blank slate. They brings fatigue from home, stress from family, pride from years of experience, and sometimes the weight of expectations from supervisors. All that plays into how he performs in the moment.

That's why safety isn't just technical, it's human. When we understand that, we stop designing systems that assume perfection. Instead, we design systems that expect imperfection and still protect people. We make it easy to do the right thing, and hard to do the wrong thing. We reward honesty, not bravado. We value clarity over speed. We create an environment where people know their limits and respect them.

Fatigue and Distraction

Fatigue is one of the most underestimated hazards in electrical work. I've seen men and women who could recite NFPA 70E cover to cover make critical errors simply because they were running on fumes. Tired eyes miss details. Tired minds skip steps. Tired hands move too fast. And distraction works the same way. A phone call from home, pressure from a boss, or an argument with a coworker can all create openings for error.

You don't solve fatigue and distraction with more rules you solve it with culture. A culture that recognizes when someone isn't fit for duty. A culture that gives space to say, "I'm not good right now." A culture that values rotating tasks, taking breaks, and pulling someone aside when their head isn't in it. That's real safety, because it protects people not just from voltage and current, but from themselves.

Pride and Ego

Pride is another hidden hazard. I've seen good hands refuse to ask for help because they didn't want to look weak. I've seen veterans skip steps because they thought experience made them immune. I've seen apprentices stay silent when they don't understand something, afraid of looking dumb. Pride kills.

We fight pride with humility and clarity. We make it clear that safety isn't about proving how tough you are, it's about proving you're still here at the end of the shift. We set the expectation that asking questions is strength, not weakness. We remind people that the standard doesn't bend for ego. Electricity doesn't care how many years you've been on the tools it only cares if you respect it.

Communication and Trust

No safety system works without communication. Peer checks, prejob briefs, and last quiet seconds all depend on people talking to each other. But communication isn't just about words, it's about trust. If I don't trust that you'll listen when I speak up, I won't say anything. If you don't trust that I'll respect your concerns, you won't raise them. And then silence sets in and silence kills.

Building trust takes time, but it starts with leaders modeling honesty. When a foreman admits his own mistake, it gives permission for everyone else to do the same. When a journeyman listens to an apprentice's concern, it tells the crew that every voice matters. Trust grows when honesty is rewarded, not punished.

Recovery and Resilience

Finally, error prevention is never complete without recovery planning. No matter how strong the system is, mistakes will happen. The question is: do they kill us, or do we survive them? Crews that rehearse recovery what to do when the unexpected happens—are the crews that live to learn from it. Recovery doesn't defeat it's discipline. It's acknowledging that we're human and building resilience in our work.

# Chapter 4

## Electrical Safety Program

"An ounce of prevention is worth a pound of cure."

— Benjamin Franklin

# Chapter 4

The transition from mindset, culture, and error prevention into a formalized Electrical Safety Program (ESP) marks a turning point in how an organization approaches risk. While individuals and crews can practice discipline on the job site, it is the Electrical Safety Program that sets the structure, defines the expectations, and provides accountability from the top down. NFPA 70E Article 110 makes it clear that employers are required to establish and document an ESP, and OSHA regulations echo this duty by requiring written programs that protect workers from recognized hazards.

An ESP is more than paperwork. It is the codification of everything we say in the field about slowing down, verifying, and building culture into a set of rules, roles, and procedures that can survive changes in leadership or turnover in the crew. Without a written program, good practices are left to memory and personal habits. With a program, they become organizational commitments that endure beyond any one person's influence. This permanence is why NFPA 70E stresses that the first priority of any ESP is hazard elimination.

The structure of an ESP generally includes several key components. First is the scope and purpose: the document must define where it applies, what hazards it covers, and why it exists. Second are roles and responsibilities. A solid program makes it clear who is responsible for implementing procedures, who authorizes energized work, and how accountability flows from management to field-level electricians. Third are the procedures themselves, from lockout/tagout to job briefings to arc flash analysis requirements. Finally, an ESP must address training, auditing, and continuous improvement, ensuring that the program does not become stale or obsolete.

A common failure of safety programs is that they become "binder ware" documents that exist in a three-ring binder on a shelf but have little influence on the day-to-day work. Crews can smell this failure instantly. When the rules on paper don't match the expectations in practice, culture collapses. The opposite is also true: when leadership models the procedures, enforces them fairly, and resources them properly, the ESP becomes a living system. Workers begin to believe the program matters because they see it applied consistently.

OSHA provides the enforcement backdrop. Standards like 29 CFR 1910.333 and 1910.147 require employers to establish safe work practices and control hazardous energy. These align directly with NFPA 70E Article 110, which demands that employers place hazard elimination as the first priority. For example, if conductors can be de-energized, they must be. Energized work is only justified under specific, documented conditions, and the ESP should spell out how those decisions are made and approved. This formal process protects not only the worker but also the employer, demonstrating due diligence and compliance with both OSHA and NFPA expectations.

Implementation requires more than writing. Rolling out an ESP is an exercise in leadership. A program launch should involve communication sessions where management explains not just what the program says but why it matters. Crews need to see how the program aligns with the values we already discussed in Chapters 1 through 3: protecting life, building culture, and designing against error. When workers recognize their own lived experience in the written document, buy-in increases.

Another critical element is auditing. NFPA 70E requires that electrical safety programs be audited at least every three years, but effective organizations audit more frequently. Audits verify not only compliance but effectiveness. They ask: Are people following the steps? Do the steps work in real-world conditions? Are there new hazards or technologies that require updates to the program? By committing to honest audits, leaders show that the ESP is dynamic, capable of growth, and responsive to changing conditions.

No ESP succeeds without resources. Leaders must provide proper PPE, training time, and qualified supervision to support the written program. If the book says one thing but the budget says another, credibility is lost. An effective ESP must be funded, staffed, and enforced if it is to have any hope of reducing risk in the field.

But beyond structure and compliance, the heart of an ESP lies in its ability to reflect the values of the organization. It must be more than a checklist, must be a living document that embodies the belief that every life matters. That belief must be visible in how we train, how we respond to incidents, and how we empower our crews to speak up. Safety is not just a rule, it's a relationship. It's the trust between leadership and labor that says, "We've got your back."

In my experience, the most effective ESPs are those that are built collaboratively. When field electricians have a voice in shaping the procedures, the program gains credibility. When supervisors listen to feedback and adjust protocols based on real-world conditions, the program becomes resilient. And when leadership treats safety as a shared responsibility—not a top-down mandate the culture begins to shift.

We must also recognize that safety programs are not static. Technology evolves. Hazards change. Crews rotate. What worked last year may not work today. That's why continuous improvement is not just a best practice, it's a survival strategy. Leaders must commit to revisiting the ESP regularly, incorporating lessons learned, and staying ahead of emerging risks.

Training is another cornerstone. A written program is meaningless if workers don't understand it. Training must be practical, relevant, and ongoing. It must go beyond the classroom and into the field, reinforcing procedures through mentorship and modeling. And it must be inclusive, ensuring that every worker regardless of experience level feels equipped to make safe decisions.

Finally, we must talk about accountability. An ESP without enforcement is just a suggestion. Leaders must be willing to hold themselves and others to the standard. That means conducting fair investigations, applying consequences consistently, and recognizing those who uphold the program with excellence. Accountability is not about punishment, it's about integrity. It's about honoring the commitment we've made to protect each other.

the Electrical Safety Program is not just a document, it's a declaration. It says, "We value life. We believe in prevention. We are committed to doing it right." When built with care, implemented with integrity, and sustained through leadership, an ESP becomes more than a compliance tool it becomes a cornerstone of culture.

And that culture is what keeps us grounded for life.

Training: Building Competency and Confidence

Training is the heartbeat of any Electrical Safety Program. It's not just about checking boxes or passing quizzes it's about building realworld competency and confidence. In my experience, the most effective training programs are those that connect the dots between policy and practice. They don't just teach what the rules are, they explain why they matter and how they save lives.

Every worker, from apprentice to master electrician, must understand the hazards they face and the controls in order to protect them. That means training must be tailored, relevant, and ongoing. A one-time orientation isn't enough. We need refresher courses, hands-on simulations, and scenario-based learning that reflects the realities of the field.

NFPA 70E requires that employees be trained to understand the specific hazards associated with electrical energy, the safe work practices required to mitigate those hazards, and the procedures for responding to incidents. OSHA echoes this in 29 CFR 1910.332, mandating training for employees who face a risk of electric shock.

But beyond compliance, training is about culture. When workers feel equipped and empowered, they're more likely to speak up, follow procedures, and look out for each other. That's why I advocate for training that's interactive, inclusive, and led by experienced professionals who've walked the walk.

Training should also include leadership development. Foremen and supervisors need to know how to coach, correct, and communicate effectively. They're the ones setting the tone on the jobsite, and their ability to reinforce safety principles is critical.

In my programs, we use a mix of classroom instruction, field demonstrations, and peer mentoring. We track progress, solicit feedback, and adjust based on what's working. Because at the end of the day, training isn't a product, it's a process. And it's one of the most powerful tools we have to protect our people.

Auditing: Accountability and Continuous Improvement

Auditing is where the rubber meets the road. It's how we verify that our Electrical Safety Program isn't just a document—it's a living, breathing system that's being followed in the field. I've seen too many companies create beautiful binders that sit on shelves while unsafe practices continue unchecked. That's not safe, that's theater.

A proper audit looks at both compliance and culture. Are procedures being followed? Are workers using the right PPE? Are permits being issued and reviewed? Are leaders reinforcing the program or undermining it? These are the questions we need to ask not just once a year, but regularly and rigorously.

NFPA 70E recommends that electrical safety programs be audited at least once every three years, but I believe in more frequent internal reviews. Monthly site inspections, quarterly program evaluations, and annual third-party audits create a rhythm of accountability that drives improvement.

Audits should be transparent and constructive. They're not about punishment, they're about progress. When we identify gaps, we address them. When we see excellence, we celebrate it. And when we find systemic issues, we dig deep to understand the root causes.

Documentation is key. Every audit should result in a report that outlines findings, corrective actions, and timelines. That report should be shared with leadership and used to inform training, updates, and strategic planning.

Most importantly, audits should involve the workforce. When workers are part of the process, they take ownership. They offer insights, raise concerns, and help shape solutions. That's how we build a culture of safety not from the top down, but from the ground up.

In my experience, the best safety programs are those that embrace auditing as a tool for learning, not just compliance. They use it to refine their approach, reinforce their values, and commit to the mission of sending every worker home safely.

Personal Leadership Stories

I remember a time early in my career when I was tasked with leading a crew through a high-voltage shutdown. The stakes were high, and the margin for error was zero. Before we even stepped onto the site, I gathered the team for a full-day training session—not just on procedures, but on mindset. We walked through every step, every contingency, and every potential hazard. That day, I saw confidence grow in my crew. When the shutdown happened, it went flawlessly. Not because we were lucky, but because we were prepared. That experience taught me that training isn't just about compliance, it's about building trust and competence.

Another moment that stood out was during an audit of a remote job site. I arrived unannounced and found a crew working without proper lockout/tagout procedures. Instead of reprimanding them on the spot, I pulled the foreman aside and asked him to walk me through his understanding of the protocol. It became clear that the training hadn't stuck. So, we paused the job, gathered the crew, and turned that audit into a teachable moment. We reviewed the procedures, discussed the risks, and made sure everyone understood the 'why' behind the rules. That day, the crew didn't just learn they took ownership. And that's the power of leadership in auditing.

Leadership isn't about being the loudest voice—it's about being the most consistent. I've made it a point to show up for every training session, not just as a speaker but as a participant. When your crew sees you learning alongside them, it sends a message: safety is everyone's responsibility. One of the most impactful moments came when a young apprentice asked me why I still attend basic safety refreshers. I told him, 'Because the day I think I know it all is the day I become a liability.' That conversation stuck with him and with me. Leadership is about modeling humility and commitment.

Responsible Parties: Roles and Accountability in Electrical Safety

In any Electrical Safety Program (ESP), clarity around roles and responsibilities is non-negotiable. If accountability is vague, safety becomes optional and that's a risk no contractor can afford. From the top down, every person involved in electrical work must understand their duties, their authority, and the consequences of inaction.

**Executive Leadership** sets the tone. If the CEO or owner doesn't prioritize safety, no one else will. Their role isn't just to approve budgets, it's to champion the culture. They must ensure the ESP is not only funded but enforced. They're responsible for empowering safety managers, supporting training initiatives, and holding the organization accountable when standards slip.

**Safety Directors and Managers** are the architects of the program. They interpret NFPA 70E, OSHA regulations, and company policy to build a framework that protects workers. But their job isn't just paperwork, it's presence. They must be visible on jobsites, accessible to crews, and relentless in their pursuit of hazard elimination. They're responsible for audits, incident investigations, and continuous improvement.

**Superintendents and Foremen** carry the program into the field. They're the bridge between policy and practice. If they don't believe in the ESP, it dies on the jobsite. These leaders must model safe behavior, enforce lockout/tagout procedures, and stop work when conditions aren't right. They're responsible for mentoring apprentices, reporting near misses, and ensuring energized work is never justified without proper documentation.

**Qualified Electrical Workers** are the front line. They must understand the hazards, follow procedures, and speak up when something's wrong. Their role isn't passive, it's proactive. They're responsible for verifying voltage absence, using PPE correctly, and refusing unsafe tasks. They must know their rights and responsibilities under the ESP and be empowered to act without fear of retaliation.

**Apprentices and Helpers** may not be qualified yet, but they're still responsible. Their role is to learn, observe, and ask questions. They must never be placed in situations beyond their training. Foremen and journeymen are responsible for their supervision, ensuring they're never exposed to energized conductors or equipment without proper oversight.

**Project Managers and Estimators** influence safety long before boots hit the ground. Their decisions around scope, schedule, and budget directly impact risk. If they underbid labor or compress timelines, they create pressure that leads to shortcuts. They're responsible for integrating safety into planning, ensuring adequate resources, and communicating expectations clearly.

**Third-Party Inspectors and Engineers** also play a role. Their designs and approvals must align with safety standards. If a spec calls for energized commissioning without justification, it must be challenged. Everyone involved in the ESP must be willing to speak up—even when it's uncomfortable.

Ultimately, accountability means consequences. If someone ignores a safety protocol, there must be follow-up. If a leader fails to act on a hazard report, there must be escalation. An ESP without enforcement is just a binder on a shelf. But when roles are clear, and accountability is real, safety becomes part of the culture, not just a compliance checkbox.

This clarity of responsibility is what separates reactive programs from resilient ones. And in my experience, the most successful contractors are the ones who treat every role no matter how small as essential to survival.

### Hazard Elimination: The First Line of Defense

When it comes to electrical safety, hazard elimination isn't just a best practice—it's the gold standard. It's the first question we ask before any energized work is considered: Can this hazard be removed entirely? If the answer is yes, then that's the path we take. No exceptions. No shortcuts.

I've always told my crews, "If you can eliminate the hazard, you eliminate the risk." That mindset must be ingrained at every level—from the apprentice pulling wire to the executive signing off on budgets. Hazard elimination is not a luxury; it's a leadership responsibility.

#### Strategies for Elimination

Elimination starts with design. If we can engineer out the hazard before the first tool hits the ground, we're ahead of the game. That means specifying equipment that allows for de-energized maintenance, using remote racking systems, and designing layouts that minimize exposure.

Next comes planning. Job hazard analysis (JHA) must be thorough and honest. We don't pencil-whip these forms we use them to identify every potential hazard and ask the hard questions: Can this be done differently? Can we schedule downtime to de-energize? Can we use alternate methods?

Then there's execution. Lockout/tagout (LOTO) procedures must be followed to the letter. Verification of zero energy state isn't optional, it's mandatory. And if there's any doubt, we stop. Because in our world, hesitation saves lives.

#### Justification Protocols for Energized Work

Sometimes, elimination isn't possible. Critical systems can't be shut down, or the risk of de-energizing exceeds the risk of working live. In those rare cases, energized work must be justified—and that justification must be documented, reviewed, and approved by leadership.

I've denied energized work requests that didn't meet the standard. I've challenged engineers to rethink their designs. I've pushed back on clients who wanted speed over safety. Because leadership means making the hard calls and standing by them.

Leadership Responsibilities

Hazard elimination is a leadership issue. It's about setting expectations, allocating resources, and holding the line. Leaders must ensure that elimination is the first option considered not the last. They must empower their teams to speak up, stop work, and demand safer alternatives.

Training plays a role here too. Leaders must be educated on the principles of hazard elimination, not just the compliance checkboxes. They must understand the cost of failure—not just in dollars but in lives.

And most importantly, they must model the behavior. If a foreman skips LOTO, the crew will follow. If a superintendent shrugs off a JHA, the culture erodes. But if a leader insists on elimination, even when it's inconvenient, that message sticks.

Hazard elimination isn't just a technical strategy, it's a cultural one. And it starts at the top.

Closing Summary

As we close Chapter 4, it's clear that an Electrical Safety Program is far more than a binder on a shelf—it's a living, breathing system that protects lives. Its structure must be intentional, its leadership unwavering, and its execution relentless. From the boardroom to the breakroom, every responsible party must understand their role in shaping a culture of safety. Training isn't just about compliance, it's about building confidence, competence, and character. Auditing isn't about catching mistakes it's about reinforcing accountability and driving continuous improvement. Hazard elimination must be the first instinct, not the last resort. And when energized work is justified, it must be backed by preparation, documentation, and leadership that refuses to compromise. This chapter is a call to action for every contractor, supervisor, and safety professional: own your role, lead with integrity, and never forget that the decisions you make today shape the legacy you leave tomorrow. Grounded for life means grounded in purpose, grounded in truth, and grounded in the belief that safety is not just a priority, it's a way of life.

Chapter 5

Training, Certification, and Competency

"An investment in knowledge pays the best interest."
— Benjamin Franklin

# Chapter 5

I've been around long enough to know this: you can hand a man the best tools in the catalog, give him brand-new PPE, stack a bookshelf with binders of procedures, and it won't mean a thing if he doesn't have the training to back it up. Gear without training is just window dressing. Rules without competency are just words on paper. At the end of the day, the only thing standing between a worker and a casket is the training that lives in his head and the habits that live in his hands.

I've walked onto jobs where training was treated like a chore, something to rush through so production wouldn't slow down. I've also walked onto jobs where training was sacred, where crews drilled like soldiers, where nobody touched a panel without proving they knew their stuff. The difference between those jobs was the difference between a safe shift and an accident waiting to happen.

The law backs me up here. OSHA says flat out in 29 CFR 1910.332: if you face electrical risk, you must be trained in and familiar with the safety practices that apply to your job. NFPA 70E takes it further and defines "qualified" as not just someone who sat in a classroom, but someone who has demonstrated real-world skills and knowledge and can identify and avoid hazards. That's not fluff. Those definitions were written in blood.

But let me step outside the standards for a moment. Training is not a class. Training is not a card in your wallet. Training is not a sign-off sheet. Training is what kicks in when your adrenaline spikes and your brain wants to skip steps. Training is that little voice that makes you pause before you touch the conductor, that habit that makes you test your tester, that discipline that forces you to verify one more time before contact. If that voice isn't there, the binder in the office won't save you.

Qualified vs. Unqualified

This trade lives and dies on one line: qualified vs. unqualified. NFPA 70E says it plain: qualified means proven skills, proven knowledge, and proper training. Unqualified means you don't have it. No middle ground.

But I've seen that line blurred too many times. I've seen foremen shove apprentices into live gear because they were shorthanded. I've seen supervisors convince themselves that "he's been here long enough; he'll figure it out." And I've seen that decision almost kill people.

One job sticks with me. A sharp apprentice, eager to prove himself, was handed live 480 to troubleshoot. He trusted his foreman's judgment. His hands were shaking, sweat dripping down his face. I saw it happening, and someone yanked him out before he crossed conductors. If he hadn't, we'd have planned a funeral. That's what happens when leaders forget the line between qualified and unqualified. That's not leadership that's betrayal.

And let me be clear: experience doesn't freeze time. A 30-year electrician who hasn't retrained on arc-flash boundaries or new PPE standards isn't qualified for today's work. Qualification isn't a badge you earn once. It's something you prove repeatedly.

Training as a Living Process

NFPA 70E says retrain at least every three years, sooner if there's a problem. Some guys roll their eyes at that. They think once they've got it, they've got it for life. That's not reality. Skills fade. Habits decay. Complacency seeps in.

I've watched seasoned electricians skip verifying their testers because "they've done it a thousand times." One day, the tester was faulty. He swore the circuit was dead. If I hadn't stopped the job, the apprentice beside him would've put his hands into live parts. That wasn't a rookie mistake. That was a veteran who let his habits rot. That's why retraining matters. It puts the basics back in front of you. It reminds you why those little steps are life and death.

Retraining isn't punishment. It's a reset button. It keeps your edge sharp. It keeps the basics alive when repetition makes you lazy. Every time technology changes, every time standards shift, every time a near-miss tells us we're slipping retraining is how we stay in the fight.

Certifications — Milestones, Not Finish Lines

I've earned my share of certifications. CESCP. OSHA Outreach. NCCER instructor. Each one cost me sweat, late nights, and effort. I'm proud of them. But let me tell you this: those cards won't save me in front of a live panel.

I've seen managers wave their certificates like armor while their crew cut corners. A certificate doesn't stop an arc flash. A laminated card doesn't ground a circuit. A framed credential doesn't walk you home. Certifications matter because they prove commitment and open doors. They're milestones, not finish lines.

I tell crews this straight: your real certification isn't the paper in your wallet. It's whether you lock and tag every single time. It's whether you verify your meter before you trust it. It's whether you walk away from the job alive. That's the certification I care about.

Training Must Be Real

I've sat through training that was a joke. PowerPoint slides. Halfasleep instructors. A quiz at the end that you could guess your way through. That kind of training is worse than none, because it gives people false confidence.

Real training is sweat. Real training is practice. Real training is putting on your arc suit, pulling open a panel, and walking through the steps with someone watching you. It's being forced to call out your actions. It's being corrected when you cut corners. It's repeating it until it becomes habit.

I've trained apprentices who could ace a written test but froze the first time they stood in front of live gear. That's because knowledge without practice is useless. Real training blends the classroom with the field until the two can't be separated.

Documentation — Proof and Protection

Nobody likes paperwork. But documentation is survival. OSHA and NFPA both demand it. If training isn't documented, in the eyes of the law, it didn't happen.

I've sat in investigations after incidents. When the training records were solid, the company showed they had done their part. When the records were missing, the company was shredded. Documentation protects the company, but it also protects the crew. It proves the investment was real.

And let me say this as plain as I can: falsifying records is worse than not training at all. Signing off someone as trained when they are not handing them a loaded gun with the safety off. That's not just negligence. That's a death sentence waiting to be carried out.

Leadership's Responsibility

Training doesn't end in the classroom. It lives in the field. I've worked for leaders who thought training was HR's problem and their only job was to push production. Those leaders built unsafe crews. I've also worked for leaders who treated every task as training. They stopped working to coach. They drilled their crews. They modeled safety. Those leaders-built teams you could trust with your life.

If you're a leader, know this: your crew is watching you. They will copy what you do. If you cut corners, they will cut corners. If you wear your PPE, they will wear theirs. If you lock out, they will lock out. Leadership is training in its most powerful form.

A real leader doesn't just hand out tasks. A real leader shapes habits. He corrects mistakes. He demands retraining when it's needed. He proves every day that safety isn't optional — it's the standard.

Training Is an investment

I've heard it all. "Training costs too much." "We can't afford the downtime." "We'll just show them on the floor." Every company that talks like that ends up paying more in one incident than they ever would have spent on training.

Franklin said knowledge pays the best interest. He was right. In this trade, the dividends are lives saved, downtime avoided, and reputations protected. Training isn't a cost. It's the cheapest insurance you'll ever buy. The trained crew is a safe crew. A safe crew is a productive crew. That's the return.

The Human Side of Competency

Competency isn't just technical. It's human. I've watched apprentices transform when training finally clicked. The moment they realized their lockout, their test, their PPE wasn't just for compliance   it was for survival. That's when they grew from workers into tradesmen.

Competency builds confidence, but not arrogance. The competent worker admits when he doesn't know. He asks questions. He raises his hand when something feels wrong. That humility keeps him alive.

Pride kills. I've seen men too proud to admit they were tired, too proud to ask for help, too proud to admit they didn't understand. Training smashes that pride and replaces it with professionalism. Competency gives a man the courage to tell the truth, even when it costs him face.

And let's not ignore fatigue and distraction. I've seen brilliant men make stupid mistakes because they were exhausted or their head was somewhere else. Competent crews watch each other. They don't just check PPE. They check each other's state. If a man is off his game, they pause. That's competency too — knowing when to step back and when to step in.

Conclusion

Training, certification, and competency aren't bureaucracy. They're survival. They're the difference between burying a brother and buying him a beer after shift. They're the difference between a reputation for safety and a headline about tragedy.

I've also watched trained crews walk away from near misses unharmed because their training kicked in at the right time. That's the difference.

Training isn't optional. Certification isn't immunity. Competency isn't a certificate. These are the lifelines of our trade. Ignore them, and you'll pay the price. Live them, and you'll build a career worth having.

Franklin was right. Knowledge pays the best interest. In this trade, that interest is measured in lives, families, and futures. If we invest in training with the same seriousness we invest in production, then we're not just building projects. We're building lives that last.

When Training Fails

I can't count the number of times I've stepped onto a site after an incident and found that training had failed long before the accident ever happened. It wasn't that the crew didn't care. It was that they were never prepared for the exact moment they faced. They'd had the slideshow, they'd signed the attendance sheet, but they hadn't lived the training.

Building Competency Through Repetition

Competency isn't built by hearing something once. It's built by doing it, repeatedly, until it becomes part of your muscle memory. Ask any soldier, firefighter, or lineman who's lived through high-stress moments you don't rise to the occasion, you fall back on your training.

When I train apprentices on lockout/tagout, I don't just explain it. I make them walk me through it until I could wake them up at three in the morning and they'd still know exactly how to do it. Apply the lock. Tag it. Test it. Verify. Ground if necessary. Call out every step. I've seen young men roll their eyes at the repetition, but later I've seen those same men in front of live gear, steady because their body knew what to do even when their mind was racing. That's the kind of competence that saves lives.

Pride, Ego, and the Hidden Hazards

Another killer of competency is pride. Pride whispers, "I don't need more training. I've been doing this long enough." I've seen men with decades of experience skip steps because they thought they were above it. I've seen apprentices too embarrassed to admit they didn't understand, so they stayed silent. Pride kills.

I'll never forget one foreman I worked under who used to say, "If you don't know, just figure it out." That kind of culture breeds silence and fear. Nobody wanted to look weak. And that's when mistakes piled up. Compare that to another leader I worked with years later, who told his crew, "If you don't know, speak up. That's strength." That crew was safer every single day because they were honest.

Competency isn't just skill. It's humility. It's knowing when to stop, when to ask, when to say, "I need help." Training must kill pride before pride kills people.

Leadership Makes or Breaks Training

I've said it before, and I'll keep saying it: leadership is training in its most powerful form. Crews copy their leaders. If the boss cuts corners, the crew cuts corners. If the boss locks and tags, the crew locks and tags.

I once worked at a site where the superintendent never wore his PPE. He thought he was above it. His crew followed his lead. Hard hats off, gloves off, safety glasses tucked in their pockets. It only took one accident for that site to change its tune. But by then, it was too late for the man who got hurt.

I've also seen the opposite. Leaders who carried safety into everything. Who wore their PPE, locked out every time, tested every circuit in front of their crews. They didn't just talk training — they lived it. And those crews became disciplined without even realizing it. That's the power of leadership.

## Documentation That Holds Weight

When training is challenged, the first thing investigators ask for is documentation. And I've sat in those rooms. When the records were solid dates, content, trainer's name, signatures it showed commitment. When the records were sloppy or missing, the company's credibility collapsed.

But let me stress this again: false documentation is worse than no documentation. Signing off on training that never happened is loading a gun and handing it to someone blindfolded. It's not just unethical, it's lethal. I've seen companies take that shortcut, and it always comes back to biting them.

Real documentation isn't just about compliance. It's proof that you value your people enough to track their growth, to hold them accountable, and to protect them with more than empty promises.

## When Training Saves

It's not all failure. I've seen training save lives in dramatic ways.

There was a site where an apprentice reached for a conductor he thought was dead. Right before contact, the journeyman next to him called out, "Stop! Verify!" That pause — drilled into him from years of training — gave the apprentice just enough time to realize his mistake. They tested. It was still energized. That pause saved him from electrocution.

That's what real training does. It creates habits that surface at the right time. It builds peer checks into the culture. It makes sure the last quiet second before contact is never rushed. Those small moments are the payoff for every hour spent drilling the basics.

## Fatigue and Distraction

Competency is more than skill. It's state of mind. I've seen sharp electricians turn sloppy because they were tired, distracted, or stressed out. Training must prepare workers to recognize those states in themselves and in their crew.

I once stopped a man from working live because I could see his hands trembling. He was exhausted, working his third 12-hour shift in a row. He swore he was fine. I told him straight: "You're not. Sit down." He argued but later admitted he couldn't remember half the steps he'd been about to take. Fatigue makes you forget the basics. And forgetting the basics is how people die.

That's why competent crews watch each other. They don't just check PPE. They check for signs of distraction, for fatigue, for someone rushing or zoning out. That's competency to protecting each other when pride won't let someone admit they're off their game.

Investment in Training Pays Back

I've seen companies cut training budgets to save a buck, and I've seen those same companies lose ten times that amount after one accident. Equipment damage. OSHA fines. Lawsuits. Lost contracts. And worst of all, broken families.

Training costs time and money, but the return on that investment is measured in lives and futures. I've never once seen a company regret training its people properly. I've seen plenty regret not doing it.

The Survival Guide Lesson

This isn't theory. It's survival. Training, certification, and competency aren't boxes to check. They're lifelines. They're how we bury pride, fight complacency, and protect each other in a trade that doesn't forgive mistakes.

I've watched trained crews stop near misses before they turned into funerals. That's why I keep preaching it. That's why I'll never stop.

Training is survival. Certification is proof of progress, not immunity. Competency is the measure that decides whether you walk away from the panel or not. Franklin was right — knowledge pays the best interest. In our world, it pays with lives saved, families kept whole, and futures protected.

Chapter 6

Hazard Recognition and Risk    Assessment in Electrical Work

"An ounce of prevention is worth a pound of cure."
— Benjamin Franklin

Survival in this trade is not about luck or shortcuts. The lesson of this chapter is clear: discipline, culture, and respect for the hazard are the only shields that last. Every page written here carries the same truth — those who follow the steps with honesty go home; those who gamble with energy or neglect the basics do not. Remember: survival isn't dramatic, it's deliberate. Carry this mindset forward into the next chapter, and into every shift you work.

# Chapter 6

## Introduction

Electricity doesn't care who you are. It doesn't matter how many years you've been on the job, how tired you are, or what your production deadlines look like. It is constant, unforgiving, and always waiting for a lapse in judgment. That's why hazard recognition and risk assessment aren't just part of the job they are the job. They're the first defense between going home safe and becoming a statistic.

Too often, people think of hazard recognition as paperwork. They picture a form, a few boxes checked, and a signature before moving on. But the truth is, hazard recognition is a mindset. Its eyes open, brain engaged, and discipline sharpened. Risk assessment is the companion: not only seeing what's dangerous, but measuring its severity, evaluating the likelihood of harm, and putting controls in place before the hazard takes control of you.

In electrical work, these habits are non-negotiable. From 120-volt receptacles in an office space to 13.8-kilovolt switchgear in a utility yard, hazard recognition is what allows us to survive long enough to build, maintain, and retire with our health intact.

## Why Hazard Recognition Matters

Most electrical incidents don't come out of nowhere. They are almost always preceded by a visible hazard that was either ignored or never seen. A mislabeled breaker. A missing panel cover. An extension cord worn down to bare copper. A combiner box left open in the rain. These aren't "accidents." They are hazards that should have been recognized and controlled.

The tragedy is that in most cases, someone walked past those hazards and didn't act. Fatigue, production pressure, pride, or plain complacency blinded them. Hazard recognition isn't about extraordinary vision. It's about slowing down long enough to see what's right in front of you.

And here's the hard truth: the hazard doesn't go away because you don't acknowledge it. It waits. It waits until you're rushed, until you're tired, until you forget the basics. That's when it strikes.

The Human Factor

Human beings are wired for routine. The more often we do something without incident, the more we believe it will always be safe. That's where hazard recognition fails.

I've seen men breeze past "Danger — High Voltage" signs because they've opened the same panel a hundred times before. I've seen apprentices hesitate to ask questions because they didn't want to look inexperienced. I've seen veterans cut corners because they believed their decades in the trade gave them immunity. Every one of those behaviors erodes hazard recognition.

Recognizing hazards requires humility. You must admit that you are not above risk. You must accept that every panel, every conductor, every piece of equipment deserves the same deliberate attention. When you drop that humility, you stop seeing. And when you stop seeing, the hazard wins.

Common Electrical Hazards

In electrical work, hazards are not mysteries. They show up in recognizable forms every single day:

Exposed Conductors — Open junction boxes, damaged insulation, missing panel covers.

Improper Grounding — Floating neutrals, disconnected bonds, makeshift grounds that create shock paths.

Overloaded Equipment — Breakers doubled up, cords daisy-chained, panels running hot.

Defective Tools — Damaged extension cords, worn-out meters, screwdrivers with insulation missing.

Arc Flash Potential — High fault current gear, equipment with no updated labels, switchgear lacking arc-resistant design.

Solar Hazards — Poorly labeled strings, DC disconnects left energized, combiner boxes exposed to weather.

Environmental Factors — Wet conditions, poor lighting, confined spaces with energized parts.

Every one of these is a red flag waving for attention. Training teaches you to look for them. Competency comes from developing the habit of never walking past them.

Risk Assessment — Seeing Beyond the Hazard

Recognition is step one. Risk assessment is step two. NFPA 70E makes it clear: before you interact with electrical parts, you must assess the risk.

Risk assessment asks two questions:

What's the worst that can happen? (severity)

How likely is it? (probability)

In our line of work, "worst case" often means fatality. That's not exaggeration it's physics. A misstep around energized conductors can end a life in milliseconds. So when risk assessment shows both high severity and realistic probability, that risk is unacceptable until controls are in place.

A true risk assessment considers:

Voltage level and available fault current.

Arc flash boundary and shock approach distances.

Condition of the equipment.

Human factors — worker training, fatigue, distractions.

Jobsite environment — wet floors, cramped spaces, poor lighting.

The point of risk assessment isn't to scare people. It's to give clarity. If you understand the risk in front of you, you can apply the right level of control.

The Hierarchy of Controls in Electrical Work

Controls aren't all equal. The hierarchy of controls sets the priority:

Elimination — Shut it down. De-energize. Establish an electrically safe work condition. This is the gold standard.

Substitution — Less common in electrical work, but sometimes possible (e.g., using battery-powered tools instead of corded ones).

Engineering Controls — Interlocks, physical barriers, GFCIs, insulation, arc-resistant gear. These protect you by design.

Administrative Controls — Job safety planning, energized work permits, LOTO procedures, pre-job briefs. These manage human behavior.

PPE — The last defense. Arc-rated suits, voltage-rated gloves, hoods, face shields. PPE won't prevent the incident — it just reduces the damage if everything else fails.

I tell every crew: if the only thing keeping you alive is your PPE, you've already lost the higher fight. PPE buys you a chance, not immunity.

Training Hazard Recognition

Hazard recognition isn't instinct — it's taught, practiced, and reinforced. A structured program for training looks like this:

Initial Instruction — Workers learn types of hazards, NFPA 70E categories, OSHA requirements, and the hierarchy of controls.

Hands-On Walkdowns — Crews Walk through facilities with mentors and are challenged to point out hazards.

Repetition and Drills — Spotting hazards become part of daily warm-ups, safety talks, and JHAs.

Peer Verification — Teams are trained to double-check each other before starting work.

Retraining Cycles — Workers are refreshed at least every three years, sooner if gaps appear.

Training also needs to use real equipment. Nothing replaces walking into a mechanical room, opening a panel, and being asked: "What do you see?" That repetition creates eyes that never stop scanning.

Going Deeper: Electrical-Specific Training Electrical

hazard recognition training must cover:

Arc flash and shock boundaries.

Proper approach distances for qualified vs. unqualified workers.

Lockout/tagout procedures with full demonstration.

Energized work permit requirements.

Identifying faulty tools and defective PPE.

Reading and interpreting one-line diagrams for hazard planning.

The goal is not memorization. The goal is instinct. When a worker can glance at equipment and immediately know where the hazards are, training has succeeded.

Training Risk Assessment

Risk assessment isn't just for supervisors. Every electrician must be able to do it in real time.

Effective training should include:

Job Hazard Analysis (JHA) Breaking down each task into steps and identifying hazards at every stage.

Scenario-Based Drills — Walking through "what-if" scenarios (e.g., testing a motor circuit, resetting a breaker, working in a wet environment).

Boundary Setup — Practicing how to physically mark off arc flash and shock boundaries.

Permit Training — Learning to fill out energized work permits correctly, understanding that these are accountability tools, not permission slips.

The goal is simple: no one should touch a panel, or a switch gear until they've run the mental checklist — what are the hazards, what's the risk, and what's my control?

Leadership's Role

Hazard recognition and risk assessment depend heavily on leadership. Leaders set the tone.

Leaders who rush production teach crews to ignore hazards.

Leaders who falsify documentation teach crews that safety is a joke.

Leaders who model vigilance teach crews to respect hazards.

Strong leaders:

Hold meaningful pre-job briefs where hazards are openly discussed.

Demand that lockout/tagout is followed without exception.

Call out complacency immediately.

Encourage questions and never punish workers for speaking up.

Schedule retraining when gaps are exposed.

Walk the site themselves, pointing out hazards to reinforce the culture.

Weak leaders, by contrast, let hazards become background noise. Crews under weak leadership stop looking. Crews under strong leadership never stop scanning.

### Fighting Complacency

Complacency is the silent killer. It sets in when workers repeat the same tasks until they stop paying attention.

Leadership must actively combat complacency with:

Safety Stand-Downs — Pausing work to refresh basics.

Near-Miss Reviews — Treating close calls as learning opportunities, not ignoring events.

Peer Accountability — Teaching workers to look out for each other, not just themselves.

Rotation of Tasks — Preventing routine from dulling vigilance.

Competency is more than skill — it's vigilance. And vigilance fades if it's not deliberately maintained.

### Documentation and Auditing

Training and risk assessment must be documented. OSHA and NFPA require it, but more importantly, it's proof of commitment.

Strong documentation should include:

Detailed training logs (dates, topics, trainer).

Records of individual competency tests.

Results of hazard recognition drills and JHA reviews.

Audit records showing where improvements are needed.

Audits should not be a punishment. There should be opportunities to spot weaknesses before incidents occur. Leadership must use documentation as both proof of training and a tool for continuous improvement.

Integration Into Daily Operations

Hazard recognition and risk assessment can't live in binders. They must live in daily routines:

Pre-Job Briefings — Every briefing must cover hazards, risks, and controls.

On-the-Spot Assessments — Workers stop before each new task and scan for hazards.

Team Hazard Checks — Crews call out hazards together, creating a shared awareness.

Job Closeouts — Reviewing hazards at the end of work so the next crew doesn't inherit surprises.

When hazard recognition becomes habit, complacency has no room to grow.

Conclusion

Hazard recognition and risk assessment are not optional. They are not paperwork exercises. They are survival habits in a trade that doesn't forgive mistakes.

Electricity doesn't care about excuses. It doesn't wait for you to catch up. It reacts instantly, and if you haven't trained yourself to recognize and control hazards, it will be too late.

Leaders who model vigilance create crews who survive. Training that drills hazard recognition creates instincts that protect lives. Documentation that proves competency ensures accountability. Risk assessments that are made, not just written, keep the hazard from becoming a tragedy.

Recognize the hazard. Respect the risk. Apply the control. Train until it's instinct. Lead like lives depend on them because they do.

Hazard recognition and risk assessment are the ounce of prevention Franklin wrote about. In our world, that ounce isn't just worth a pound of cure — it's worth everything.

# Chapter 7

## PPE: The last line of defense

### Epilogue — Chapter 7
Survival in this trade is not about luck or shortcuts. The lesson of this chapter is clear: discipline, culture, and respect for the hazard are the only shields that last. Every page written here carries the same truth — those who follow the steps with honesty go home; those who gamble with energy or neglect the basics do not. Remember: survival isn't dramatic, it's deliberate. Carry this mindset forward into the next chapter, and into every shift you work.

## Chapter 7

## PPE and the Illusion of Safety

In electrical work, PPE gets treated like armor—something you throw on and march into danger with. But armor doesn't make you invincible, and it never will. PPE is not your first line of defense; it's your last, and it only buys you time when everything else goes wrong. If you reach for PPE before you reach for elimination, substitution, engineering controls, and administrative discipline, you're not being brave, you're being reckless. I say that as a trainer, a contractor, and a servicemember who has stood in front of hot gear and felt the weight of that decision. I've seen the full spectrum: crews who treat PPE like a cape, and crews who treat it like a last resort. Only one of those crews survived the long game.

The hierarchy of controls is not a poster on the wall; it's a survival sequence. When we choose PPE while skipping lockout/tagout, skipping boundaries, skipping permits, or skipping a walk-down, we are quietly trading our lives for minutes on a schedule. That trade always comes due. The truth is simple: PPE is mitigation, not prevention. It reduces harm; it does not remove hazards. That difference is everything.

I've trained workers who believed arc-rated suits made them invulnerable. I've been on job sites where gloves past their test date kept getting used because "they look fine." I've watched face shields so scratched you could barely see through them get passed around as if visibility were optional. And I've heard the same three lines everywhere I go: "We've done it this way for years." "It'll just take a second." "My gear will handle it." Those aren't experiences; they're warnings.

Standards exist because people died before them. OSHA 29 CFR 1910.132 sets the foundation for personal protective equipment—assessment, provision, training, and maintenance, so employers don't rely on luck. OSHA 1910.335 speaks directly to PPE and protective tools in electrical work—what to wear, when to wear it, and what not to trust when equipment is or may be energized. NFPA 70E ties it all together by forcing the conversation we dodge to establish an Electrically Safe Work Condition first, then talk about PPE if justified energized work is truly unavoidable (NFPA 70E, 2024). Gloves are governed under ASTM F496 for testing; arc-rated clothing under ASTM F1506; arc flash face protection under ASTM F2178; and insulated hand tools under ASTM F1505. Those aren't trivia answers; they're lifelines that define how good your "last line" really is.

Culture: the Quiet Killer or the Shield We Build

Culture is how we behave when no one is watching. It shows up in the little choices: whether you air-test gloves before use, whether you clean that hood properly, whether you call out a teammate who skipped a step, whether you stop the job when your gut says something's off. A culture that treats PPE like a costume also treats risk like a rumor. That culture will eventually bury someone. A culture that treats PPE as sacred—but secondary to elimination, engineering, and administrative rigor—builds redundancy into every shift. That culture sends people home.

The psychology behind the illusion of safety is powerful. Gear feels good. It feels proactive. It quiets anxiety. Put on a 40 cal/cm² suit and your brain whispers, "You've got this." That whisper is dangerous. Psychologists call it risk compensation—the tendency to take greater risks when we feel more protected. In our world, that looks like stepping deeper into an energized cabinet because "the suit can handle it," or skipping a re-verification because "we're covered." That's how PPE, misused, becomes bait.

There's another psychological trap: habituation. Do a risky task enough times without consequence and the brain starts calling it normal. The checklist feels excessive. The boundary seems "overkill." The glove air test looks like wasted motion. That's the moment when a mature safety culture saves you—because a mature culture doesn't negotiate with what the brain normalizes. It re-anchors behavior to standards, not feelings.

Leadership sets that anchor. When supervisors wear their own PPE, air-test their own gloves, and demand ESWC before work, crews follow. When leaders quietly roll their eyes at the extra steps, crews imitate that too. People don't do what the policy says, they do what the boss honors. If you want disciplined PPE use, build visible rituals around it: pre-job glove tests, face shield checks under bright light, garment label reads before energized tasks. Make those rituals public and predictable. Reward them. Normalize them. That's how you replace the illusion of safety with the behavior of survival.

What Survival Actually Looks Like

Survival is not dramatic. It rarely looks heroic. It is boring on purpose. It looks like a worker who won't put a hand on metal until he's proved it dead with a properly rated meter, he just function-tested on a known live source. It looks like a foreman who calls a timeout because a face shield is too scratched to see through.
It looks like a crew who refuses to "make it quick" on an energized 480-V bucket because the permit isn't complete. It looks like voltage-rated gloves stored flat, away from sunlight, chemicals, and sharp edges—and rejected on the spot if ozone cracking shows up. It looks like arc-rated clothing laundered correctly, with no fabric softeners, no contamination, and no melted logos stitched where they don't belong. That's survival. It's not flashy. It's deliberate. It works.

Standards and Testing— 'Trust, but Verify'

If your gear isn't tested, it's not PPE—it's theater. Voltage-rated gloves must be lab tested every six months per ASTM F496, and air tested before each use. A pinhole can turn a routine task into a life-altering event. Arc-rated garments must meet ASTM F1506, and the label must match the incident energy or arc rating method your hazard analysis calls for—if the job is 25 cal/cm$^2$ and you're wearing a 12 cal suit, you are knowingly exposed. Face protection must meet ASTM F2178 and, when applicable, ANSI Z87.1 for impact. Insulated tools should conform to ASTM F1505 and be visually inspected every time you reach for them. None of this is optional if you're serious about living to see the next shift.

The Hierarchy of Controls—PPE Comes Last

Eliminate the hazard first. De-energize, lock, tag, try. Substitute safer methods where possible. Engineer the hazard down with physical barriers, remote racking, and permanent shutters. Apply administrative controls—permits, boundaries, documented procedures, supervision—so you're not trusting memory in a high-risk moment. Only then, if risk remains, do you pick PPE. This isn't just a model out of a textbook; it's the survival. ISO 45001 says the same thing in global language: control risks at their source before putting it on the worker's back. NFPA 70E says plainly: establish an Electrically Safe Work Condition unless you can prove you cannot. PPE is a parachute, not wings.

False Confidence vs. Useful Confidence

Confidence is not the enemy; unearned confidence is. Useful confidence is built from preparation, clear roles, rehearsed procedures, and valid PPE that you know how to inspect, don, doff, and maintain. False confidence is built from luck, shortcuts that didn't bite you yet, and suits that look tough but test weak. The first lowers risk; the second loads the chamber.

Training That Actually Changes Behavior

Issuing gear is not training. Reading a slide is not training. Training is repetition plus feedback until a behavior is automatic. Set up hands-on inspection labs where every worker has to identify defects in gloves, hoods, lenses, and garments monthly. Build fit-and-function drills: full suit on, perform a realistic task with visibility constraints, fogging, and dexterity limits. Make every energized-work simulation includes the paperwork: the permit, the risk assessment, the boundary determination, the job briefing signatures. If the forms feel like theater, rewrite them so they guide decisions. If the forms never stop a job, they're not forms; they're props.

Peer accountability is a force multiplier. Teach crews to check each other's PPE without ego: "Hey, your glove's stamp is out of date." "Your hood lens is crazed—grab the spare." "Your shirt tag doesn't match the calculated IE." Normalize those interventions. Celebrate them in front of the team. The message is simple: We protect one another here.

Maintenance: The Discipline that Saves Lives

PPE fails in two ways: slowly, from neglect, and suddenly, from misuse. Voltage-rated gloves: air-test before use, lab-test every six months, store flat, keep solvents away, replace at the first sign of ozone checking. Arc-rated apparel: wash with approved detergents, ban fabric softener, retire garments with tears, contamination, or compromised closures, and never wear flammable base layers underneath. Face shields and hoods: replace scratched lenses, store in a rigid case, clean with non-abrasive products, and never leave them baking in direct sun. Insulated tools: keep them clean, check for nicks and swelling, and segregate them from non-insulated tools so they don't get banged up in the same drawer. Keep inspection logs. Track test dates. Replace it before failure. That's what respect looks like in practice.

Case Studies: When PPE Wasn't Enough—And Why

NIOSH FACE investigations read like letters from the future, warning us what happens if we keep doing what we're doing. In one case, a worker entered a conveyor housing to clear a jam. He didn't place his own lock. Another worker, thinking the line was clear, restarted the system. PPE was present; it couldn't stop a crush hazard once motion returned. In another case, a journeyman trusted a verbal "it's dead" from a supervisor. He didn't verify with his meter. He contacted an energized bus and never got back up. PPE is not a substitute for elimination, verification, or boundaries. It is a hedge, not a cure.

Electrical-Specific Realities the Catalogs Don't Tell You

Arc-rated fabrics can ignite or continue to char if contaminated with flammable substances—oils, solvents, or untreated lint. "Tough" garments can hide UV damage and fiber breakdown that only shows up when they're stressed in an event. "Meets standard" on a box doesn't mean "matches your incident energy." And that 1000-V rating stamped on a tool? It presumes intact insulation, correct use, and a system that behaves the way the test did. Real systems arc, track, and back feed in messy ways. The catalog never promises to save you from ignoring physics.

Administrative Controls That Actually Work

Write procedures at the level your crew can use in the field—short, plain language, with photos when helpful, and specific pass/fail checks ("Reject glove if air test drops within 5 seconds"). Build pre-job briefings that require each person to voice their task and hazard. Put a stop-work card in every pocket and back it with leadership that honors it. Tie replacements to the budget—don't wait for a failure. If a worker asks for new PPE, treat that as hazard communication and respond in hours, not weeks.

Legal and Economic Reality

OSHA citations for serious and willful violations involving PPE and electrical safe work practices can reach six figures. Civil litigation multiplies that. Insurance premiums have risen for years. Production stops during investigations. Good workers leave companies that gamble with their lives. The inverse is also true: contractors who invest in real controls and reliable PPE win bids because clients, insurers, and auditors can see maturity. In hard numbers and human terms, disciplined PPE used-nested inside the hierarchy of controls—is a profit center disguised as compassion.

Military Parallels: Discipline Under Pressure

In the Army and the Navy Seabees, we lived by checklists because chaos punishes improvisation. You didn't energize or de-energize without a second set of eyes. You called out steps aloud. You documented who, what, when, and why. That discipline carries straight into civilian electrical work. When the pressure hits—late schedule, impatient client, weather window closing—discipline must hold. Gear is important. Process is decisive. That's not theory; it's survival with rank removed.

## Global Perspective

Outside the U.S., you'll find the same message written a dozen different ways. ISO 45001 emphasizes hazard control at the source and worker participation. IEC 61482-2 sets arc protective clothing requirements across international lines. The EU's PPE Regulation demands conformity assessment and traceability, so bad gear doesn't slip through. Canada's CCOHS and the UK's HSE prosecute employers who fail to isolate energy and maintain PPE. The language changes; the physics do not. Everywhere you go, electricity does the same thing to the same mistakes.

## Future of PPE Without the Hype

Smart garments can stream temperature and heart rate. Hoods can integrate heads-up displays and thermal imaging. Gloves can carry RFID tags that tie to test records. Those tools are promising, especially for large fleets. But no sensor will read a room like a craftsman who was trained to slow down, verify, and think. Technology should support discipline, not replace it. The day we treat an app like a permit is the day we start writing our incident report.

## What I Expect from a Crew—and From Myself

- We eliminate hazards whenever possible. If we can de-energize, we do. If we can't, we prove why not in writing and we own that choice.
- We respect boundaries. Approach and arc flash boundaries are real distances, not suggestions.
- We verify. We test our test equipment and then we test the circuit.
- We inspect PPE every time and retire it early, not late.
- We speak up for each other. If you see me miss a step, you stop me. If I see you miss a step, I stop you.
- We lead by example. Titles don't exempt anyone from locks, tags, or face shields.
- We keep records because we respect memory limits.
- We choose discipline over drama, every single time.

## Conclusion: Grounded, Not Glamorous

PPE is not a cape. It is not courage. It is a shield that works best when it rarely needs to. The real work happens long before you zip the suit: when you plan, when you lock and tag, when you verify, when you say "not today" to a rushed energized task. If all the other layers fail, your gloves, suit, and face shield may keep a tragedy from becoming a fatality. But the only reliable way home is to control the hazard, not just wear the hazard. That's the difference between looking safe and being safe.

## Culture Under Pressure: What We Do When the Clock Is Ticking

Schedules compress judgment. Clients hover. Production wants the line back yesterday. This is the real test of culture: when time is short and eyes are watching, do we still slow down to air-test every glove, swap a clouded lens, re-verify zero energy, and finish the permit? A fragile culture cracks here. A mature one gets louder: "Gloves up. Test up. Verify up." If your crew can do those three when the heat is on, you don't have a poster—you have a culture.

## The Language We Use Shapes the Risks We Take

Words are levers. When leaders call an energized job "a quick look," risk expands. When someone says "just" or "only"— "just tighten this," "only one measurement"—they're shrinking the hazard in their mind and everyone else's. Flip the language. Say the whole risk out loud: "We are entering an arc-capable space with a known IE of 23 $cal/cm^2$; we will maintain boundary, verify absence of voltage, and dress to the calculated exposure if, and only if, the permit is approved." That sentence doesn't sound heroic, but it keeps people alive.

## The Quiet Leader's Checklist (Psychological Edition)

- I remain calm under pressure. Panic is contagious; so is discipline.

- I invite challenge. If someone thinks we're skipping a step, I want them to say it out loud.

- I narrate the standard. I don't assume people remember; I speak the steps.

- I reward the slowdown. The person who calls a timeout gets thanked in front of the team.

- I close the loop. If someone asked for replacement PPE, I told them when it's ordered and when it arrives.

- I make consequences visible. We review near-misses and lessons learned without blame, with clarity.

Micro-Practices That Change Outcomes

Tiny habits protect lives: holding your face shield at arm's length under bright light before every job to spot crazing; pinching and rolling glove cuffs during air tests until you hear the leak; writing the IE and boundaries on the whiteboard at the job site; keeping a spare set of rated gloves and a new hood lens in the truck; staging a clean base layer bag for anyone caught in a contaminated shirt; and scheduling five-minute PPE huddles at mid-shift when fatigue wrecks attention. Small things done consistently beat big speeches done annually.

How We Talk About Incidents—Without Shame, Without Excuses
Shame drives silence; silence drives repeats. When we debrief an incident or a near-miss, we stick to behavior and systems, not character. We ask: What did we expect to happen? What happened? Where did the system make the wrong action easy and the right action hard? What specific change—tooling, training, staffing, supervision, or PPE—prevents this next time? We write the change, we assign an owner, and we follow up. This is not compliance theater; it's operational learning.

The Apprentices' Contract

Apprentices inherit our habits. If we teach speed, they will sprint into panels. If we teach rituals, they will repeat ritual. We owe them more than lectures. We owe them repetitions: glove tests, label checks, boundary calls, permit rehearsals. And we owe them honesty about why: not because the book says so, but because the people before us did not go home. We honor them by being the last generation to repeat their mistakes.

Closing the Gap Between Paper and Practice

Policies are the floor, not the ceiling. Walk your site and compare the written procedure to the tools on hand, the lighting, the space to work, the actual condition of PPE, and the true production pressure. If the procedure assumes a perfect world, it will fail in a real one. Rewrite it so the right thing is the easy thing. Stock duplicate PPE at the point of use. Put the glove inflator next to the panel, not locked in a cabinet fifty yards away. Make the safe choice faster than the unsafe one, and watch your metrics move for the right reasons.

Chapter 8

Lockout/Tagout (LOTO) & Control of Hazardous Energy

Epilogue — Chapter 8
Survival in this trade is not about luck or shortcuts. The lesson of this chapter is clear: discipline, culture, and respect for the hazard are the only shields that last. Every page written here carries the same truth — those who follow the steps with honesty go home; those who gamble with energy or neglect the basics do not. Remember: survival isn't dramatic, it's deliberate. Carry this mindset forward into the next chapter, and into every shift you work.

# Chapter 8

In electrical work, nothing is more unforgiving than uncontrolled energy. Lockout/Tagout (LOTO) is not just a compliance exercise, it is the difference between a worker going home alive or not at all. Every contractor must treat hazardous energy with respect, because unlike other hazards, electricity gives no second chances. The survival mindset means embracing LOTO not as red tape, but as a discipline that protects you, your crew, and the company itself.

## Why LOTO Matters for Survival

Every year, workers die because equipment thought to be deenergized came alive without warning. OSHA estimates that proper application of LOTO prevents 120 deaths and 50,000 injuries annually in the United States (OSHA, 2024). Those numbers are not abstract; they represent real tradesmen who believed a breaker was off, who trusted a verbal assurance, or who skipped one verification step. Survival in this trade means never leaving your life to assumption. Hazardous energy must be controlled, locked, and verified every single time.

Electrical contractors especially cannot afford shortcuts. An energized conductor or back fed circuit will not announce itself—it will kill instantly. The only guarantee is discipline, and that discipline is written into LOTO. In this line of work, you never get a second chance. One lapse, one assumption, one shortcut—those are all it takes to change a life forever. That's why LOTO is not paperwork; it's survival.

## Core Standards

LOTO is codified in OSHA's 29 CFR 1910.147, "The Control of Hazardous Energy," and supported by 1910.333 for electrical work. NFPA 70E expands on these standards, requiring employers and employees to establish an Electrically Safe Work Condition (ESWC) before any work begins (NFPA, 2024). Together, these rules demand that all forms of hazardous energy—electrical, mechanical, hydraulic, pneumatic, chemical, and thermal—be isolated and verified before servicing. For electricians, the focus is almost always on electrical isolation, but a survival mindset means recognizing that a conveyor belt or pressurized line can be just as deadly as a live bus bar.

LOTO standards are not about bureaucracy, they are survival checklists. They are the hard-earned lessons of tragedy, written into law. Every step represents lives lost where corners were cut. OSHA's regulations and NFPA 70E's safe work practices do not exist to slow you down; they exist to ensure you are alive to work another day.

Historical Context of LOTO

The lockout/tagout standard did not appear overnight. It was forged in blood and tragedy. Before OSHA introduced 1910.147 in 1989, hundreds of workers were killed every year when machines unexpectedly started up. The standard was born after repeated fatal incidents highlighted the lack of uniform procedures for energy isolation. One early case that shaped the rule involved a worker crushed inside a press because another employee restored power, unaware he was still inside. That story mirrors dozens of others, each one a reminder that regulations are written in the memory of the fallen.

By 1990, OSHA estimated that full compliance with 1910.147 would save nearly 120 lives annually. The standard's importance has only grown as industrial systems have become more complex and energy sources more interdependent. The evolution of NFPA 70E mirrored this progression, giving the electrical industry a workable, practical set of steps to establish an ESWC. These documents stand as both legal requirements and moral imperatives.

When we as electricians read standards, we often forget they are written because somebody didn't make it home. Every page of OSHA 1910.147 and every chapter of NFPA 70E is a gravestone turned into guidance. That's why a survival mindset means treating standards not as obstacles but as lifelines.

Step-by-Step Survival Approach

LOTO is not complicated, but it requires discipline. The essential steps every contractor must follow are:

1. **Preparation:** Identify all energy sources and understand how they are controlled. This means reviewing one-lines, schematics, and equipment manuals.

2. **Shutdown:** Power down the machine or circuit using normal operating controls.

3. **Isolation:** Physically open disconnects, breakers, or valves to stop energy flow.

4. **Lockout/Tagout:** Apply a lock and a tag at each isolation point. Each worker must use their own personal lock. Never share keys.

5. **Release Stored Energy:** Discharge capacitors, bleed down air lines, release springs, and block mechanical parts.

6. **Verification:** Test for zero energy using properly rated instruments. "Test before touch" is non-negotiable.

7. **Perform Work:** Only after all steps above are confirmed should work begin.

8. **Release from Lockout:** When work is complete, clear the area, remove tools, and ensure all personnel are accounted for before locks are removed.

Skipping any of these steps is gambling with your life. Real survival comes from doing it right every time, no matter the pressure from production or schedule.

Common Failures and Complacency

The most common causes of LOTO failures are shortcuts and complacency:

- **Group Lock Failures:** One lock applied "for the crew" instead of individual locks. If one worker is still in the equipment when the lock is removed, the results can be fatal.

- **Borrowed Keys:** Sharing or duplicating lock keys undermines the entire system.

- **Skipped Verification:** Assuming a breaker is open without testing with a meter is one of the most common fatal errors.

- **Pressure from Leadership:** Supervisors who push workers to bypass LOTO for speed are gambling with lives and company liability.

When a crew believes that "it'll be fine this time," they've already placed themselves in danger. The survival-minded contractor calls out complacency before it becomes tragedy.

Case Studies and Lessons Learned

NIOSH's Fatality Assessment and Control Evaluation (FACE) program has documented countless tragedies that came from LOTO failures. In one case, a worker at a plastics plant died after entering a machine without applying his own lock; another worker reenergized it, unaware he was inside (NIOSH FACE, 2021). In another, an electrician assumed that a breaker was open, but a mislabeled panel left him working energized. He was fatally electrocuted. Each of these cases highlights why the mantra "Test Before Touch" and "Every Lock, Every Time" must be drilled into every worker from day one.

These stories echo through every training room because they are not isolated—they are the predictable outcome of shortcuts. When we fail to respect energy, energy punishes us with no warning and no mercy.

Survival Lessons from the Field

In survival terms, the lesson is clear: treat every source of energy as if it wants you dead. Never assume, never trust a label, and never rush the process. One story still taught in many safety meetings involves a worker who locked out a disconnect but failed to realize a second feed energized the same bus. His voltage-rated gloves saved his life, but only after severe burns and months in recovery. PPE bought him time, but a proper LOTO plan would have prevented the event entirely.

Another hard-learned lesson comes from contractors who reuse tags or fail to sign and date them properly. When an outsider or another crew comes across an unmarked tag, they cannot know who applied it or whether the lock is valid. That uncertainty has led to premature re-energization—and preventable deaths. The details of a name and date may seem small, but survival often rests in the smallest steps.

Leadership and Accountability

True contractor leadership means enforcing LOTO not just as a rule, but as a value. Supervisors must model the behavior they expect—applying their own locks, refusing to cut corners, and backing up workers who take the time to follow procedure. Accountability starts at the top. When leadership treats LOTO as sacred, crews follow suit. When leadership pressures workers to skip steps, the entire system breaks down. A survival culture requires leaders who understand that every lock is a promise, and every tag is a signature of responsibility.

Field Training and Reinforcement

Training must go beyond the classroom. Crews need hands-on practice with real equipment, mock lockout stations, and scenariobased drills. Apprentices should be taught to identify energy sources, apply locks, and verify zero energy under supervision. Use realworld case studies to reinforce the consequences of failure. Incorporate peer reviews, where workers inspect each other's lockout procedures. Reinforce the mantra: "Test before touch" and "Every lock, every time." Training should be ongoing, not a one-time event. Survival depends on repetition, reinforcement, and realism.

Technical Deep Dive: Multi-Source Isolation

Modern equipment often has multiple energy feeds—electrical, hydraulic, pneumatic. Contractors must be trained to identify all sources, not just the obvious ones. Use schematics, one-line diagrams, and manufacturer manuals to trace energy paths. In one incident, a worker locked out the main disconnect but missed a secondary feed from a backup generator. The result was a near-fatal shock. Survival means tracing every wire, every valve, every pressure line. Use color-coded lockout kits and detailed isolation maps to prevent oversight.

LOTO in Confined Spaces and High-Risk Zones

LOTO procedures become even more critical in confined spaces, where escape is limited and hazards are amplified. Before entry, verify that all energy sources are isolated and locked. Use atmospheric testing to confirm no chemical or thermal hazards remain. Assign a standby attendant trained in emergency response. In high-risk zones like substations or industrial plants, double verification should be standard—two qualified workers confirming zero energy independently. Survival in these environments requires heightened discipline and layered controls.

Technology and the Future of LOTO

Advancements in technology offer new tools for LOTO enforcement. Digital lockout systems can track who applied each lock, when it was applied, and when it was removed. Smart locks with RFID or Bluetooth can prevent unauthorized removal and log activity. Mobile apps can guide workers through step-by-step procedures and store completed checklists. While technology should never replace discipline, it can enhance accountability and reduce human error.

Contractors should evaluate these tools and integrate them where appropriate.

Contractor Liability and Legal Consequences

LOTO failures carry legal consequences. OSHA citations, fines, and lawsuits can cripple a company. More importantly, the human cost—

injury or death—can never be undone. Contractors must document every lockout procedure, maintain training records, and audit compliance regularly. In court, a missing tag or incomplete checklist can be the difference between defense and negligence. Survival means protecting your crew and your company. Treat every lockout as if it will be reviewed in a courtroom—because one day, it might be.

Psychological Safety and Crew Empowerment

LOTO is not just physical, it's psychological. Workers must feel empowered to speak up, refuse unsafe tasks, and apply their locks without fear of retaliation. Psychological safety means creating a culture where every voice matters. Encourage open dialogue, reward safety interventions, and train supervisors to listen. When crews feel safe to enforce LOTO, they do. When they fear backlash, they stay silent—and silence kills. Survival depends on courage, and courage grows in a culture of respect.

Global Standards and Perspectives

While OSHA and NFPA dominate the U.S., other nations and global standards reinforce the same principles. The International Labor Organization (ILO) calls for machinery safeguards and energy isolation across all member countries. ISO 45001, the international standard for occupational health and safety, echoes the need for strict hazardous energy control. Europe's directives on machinery safety also mandate lockout procedures. The message is universal: hazardous energy kills everywhere, and survival requires control everywhere.

Military Discipline and LOTO

As a military-trained electrician, I have seen how discipline saves lives. In the Army and Navy Seabees, checklists were non-negotiable. Before energizing or de-energizing a system, procedures were called out loud, verified by a second person, and documented. That culture translates directly into LOTO in civilian life. In the field, one missed step can compromise a mission. In industry, one missed step can cost a life. The discipline drilled into service members—never assume, always verify—is the same discipline that keeps electricians alive in plants and on job sites.

Final Survival Reminder

LOTO is not paperwork. It's not bureaucracy. It's the barrier between life and death. Every lock is a lifeline. Every tag is a warning. Every verification is a shield. Contractors who treat LOTO as sacred build crews that survive. Those who treat it as optional build crews that suffer. The survival mindset means doing it right, every time, no matter what the cost. Because the cost of skipping it is everything.

To truly understand the stakes of LOTO, you must study the cases that OSHA and NIOSH investigate each year. These are not statistics, they are names, families, and futures cut short. In one NIOSH FACE report, a 34-year-old maintenance worker was killed when he entered a conveyor system without placing his own lock. Another employee, unaware he was inside, energized the system. The man was crushed instantly (NIOSH FACE, 2019). What makes this tragedy haunting is how preventable it was: a simple lock on a disco...

Another incident involved a journeyman electrician who relied on a verbal assurance from a supervisor that a circuit was dead. Trust replaced testing. When he touched the bus, it was still live. The shock was fatal. This echoes into a truth every electrician knows: electricity does not negotiate. It demands proof, not promises.

In the construction industry, another case illustrates how pressure and complacency combine to deadly effect. A contractor working on a hydraulic press was told to "hurry it up" and skipped the lockout step, relying only on shutting down the control panel. Hydraulic pressure remained in the system, and when he reached inside, the press activated. He was crushed in front of his coworkers. That single shortcut cost him his life and left an entire crew traumatized.

Each of these examples reinforces the survival mindset: shortcuts do not save time; they steal futures. If there is one lesson that repeats across every investigation, it is this: every lock matters, every time.

## The Economics of Survival: Why LOTO Makes Business Sense

Some leaders view LOTO as a burden that slows production. But the truth is that failing to follow LOTO costs far more. OSHA penalties for willful violations of 1910.147 can exceed $150,000 per incident (OSHA, 2024). Beyond fines, companies face lawsuits, skyrocketing insurance premiums, and reputational damage that can destroy contracts. A single fatality investigation can halt production for weeks or months, costing millions in lost revenue.

Insurance companies track safety records, and poor compliance history translates to higher premiums and fewer bids won. Contractors who enforce LOTO not only save lives, they protect the bottom line. From a business perspective, every lock applied is an investment in financial stability. From a moral perspective, it is priceless.

## Deep Dive: Training, Checklists, and Crew Discipline

Training is not effective unless it is repeated, reinforced, and verified. The most successful contractors treat LOTO training like a skill, not a slide deck. Apprentices rotate through mock lockout stations, practicing until it becomes second nature. Crews walk through detailed checklists before beginning work, calling out steps aloud. A sample contractor checklist may include verifying panel labeling, ensuring group lock boxes are present, and testing meters on known live circuits before verifying zero e...

Checklists are survival tools. The aviation industry has relied on them for decades to prevent disasters. In electrical work, a LOTO checklist serves the same role. It reduces reliance on memory and ensures no step is overlooked under pressure. Supervisors must enforce checklists, not as paperwork, but as lifelines. A crew disciplined in checklists is a crew that survives.

## Crew Culture: Calling Out Complacency

Survival is not just individuality's collective. A crew that looks the other way when someone skips a lock is a crew that has already failed. Psychological safety means empowering every worker, from apprentice to foreman, to speak up without fear. If a lock is missing, if a tag is incomplete, if verification was skipped, any worker must feel not only the right but the duty to stop the job. Silence in the face of shortcuts is complicity in tragedy..

Global Lessons: LOTO Beyond the U.S.

Around the world, hazardous energy has claimed lives in every industry. In Canada, the Canadian Centre for Occupational Health and Safety (CCOHS) enforces similar lockout standards. In the United Kingdom, the Health and Safety Executive (HSE) prosecutes companies who fail to isolate energy sources. One well-known HSE case involved a worker fatally injured by a conveyor system that was not locked out. The company was fined heavily, but the family paid the true price.

The universality of these standards shows that hazardous energy respects no borders. Whether under OSHA, HSE, or ISO 45001, the principles are the same: isolate, lock, verify. Survival is a global language.

The Future of LOTO: Technology, AI, and Remote Systems

Looking ahead, technology promises both opportunities and new risks. Smart locks with digital tracking are becoming more common. These systems log exactly who placed a lock, when it was applied, and when it was removed. Remote monitoring platforms can ensure that only authorized workers have clearance. Artificial intelligence may one day analyze real-time data to detect unsafe conditions and alert crews before mistakes occur.

But technology is no substitute for discipline. A Bluetooth-enabled lock still requires a worker to apply it. A digital checklist still requires honesty in completing it. The tools may evolve, but the survival mindset remains the same: no lock, no work.

Final Survival Call

Hazardous energy is relentless. It does not forgive, and it does not wait. Contractors who enforce LOTO save lives, protect livelihoods, and build cultures that endure. Those who gamble with shortcuts invite disaster. The cost of doing it right is minutes; the cost of skipping it is everything. In the end, survival depends not on luck, but on discipline.

# Chapter 9

## Continuous Improvement & Auditing – Survival in the Field

# Chapter 9

## Introduction: Survival Is a System, not a Fluke

In the trades survival doesn't happen by luck. Nobody cheats death on high-voltage systems, scaffolds, or steel for long. The men and women who walk off the site each night aren't lucky—they're disciplined. They've built survival into their DNA. They've learned that systems, audits, and accountability are the foundation of living to see tomorrow. Survival is built one habit at a time, one lesson at a time, and one improvement at a time.

In construction, there's always a silent danger waiting for the crew that lets their guard down. Complacency. Stagnation. The moment a foreman assumes yesterday's safety talk is good enough for today's job, the door cracks open for disaster. Continuous improvement closes that door and bolts it shut. Auditing makes sure it stays locked. Every crew member, from apprentices to superintendent, plays a part in that survival system. Survival is not a fluke—it's a process, a mindset, and a standard.

## Continuous Improvement in the Trades

Improvement doesn't come from head office memos or laminated posters. It happens in the dirt, during the ten-minute huddle before sunrise, or in the exhausted debrief after twelve hours on your feet. It's forged in the moments when someone speaks up, when the team adapts, when the crew refuses to repeat the same mistake twice.

Daily Improvement:
- A foreman stops a task mid-stream because the hazard analysis doesn't match the work. Instead of pushing forward, he rewrites the JHA with the crew, teaching them how survival is written in pencil, not stone.
- An apprentice spots a journeyman about to cross a barricade line. Instead of staying silent, he calls it out. That courage becomes the crew's improvement that day.

- Crews finish the shift by talking about what almost went wrong. That ten-minute reflection becomes tomorrow's survival.

Weekly Improvement:
- Supervisors rotate toolbox talks. Apprentices lead; veterans guide. This rotation builds confidence, sharpens communication, and spreads ownership.
- Crews hold end-of-week safety huddles: not about production, but about what hazards taught them. Mistakes turn into training tools. Lessons become collective, not individual.

Long-Term Improvement:
- Contractors capture lessons into binders, logs, and digital systems. That knowledge is handed to the next crew, the next site, the next generation. Survival is no longer memory—it's legacy.
- Mentorship programs pair rookies with veterans. Skills get passed down, but more importantly, so do survival habits. Veterans teach not just the 'how,' but the 'why.'

The trades are brutal teachers. The price of stagnation is injury, downtime, or worse. Crews that commit to constant sharpening thrive. Crews that coast eventually fall.

Auditing for Survival, Not Compliance

Too many people hear the word 'audit' and picture clipboards, checklists, and finger-pointing. That's not survival—that's bureaucracy. A real audit doesn't exist to catch you doing something wrong. It exists to prove that your system works when nobody's looking.

A true survival audit asks: Are we living the standard or just reciting it?

Step-by-Step Survival Audit:

1. Walk the site with humility. Show up like a teammate, not a cop.
2. Observe behavior, not just paperwork. Look at what people do when the supervisor isn't standing over them.
3. Ask open-ended questions: "How do you know this circuit is dead?" "What's your backup if this fails?"
4. Coach on the spot. Turn findings into lessons, not write-ups.
5. Document what matters. Not every detail, just the patterns that tell you where risk lives.
6. Revisit. An audit isn't finished until you confirm the lesson stuck.

Bad audits punish. Good audits protect. Great audits build trust. A survival audit is not a trap—it's a mirror. And when crews learn to see audits as allies, culture shifts. Safety becomes second nature. Improvement becomes inevitable.

Leadership and Accountability in Improvement

Systems don't drive improvement, leaders do. The way a foreman handles a near miss, the way a superintendent reacts to bad news, the way a journeyman teaches an apprentice—all of these define whether survival is just a word on a banner or a reality in the dirt.

Leadership by Example:
-   Leaders admit mistakes. A foreman who says, "That one's on me," teaches the crew that accountability isn't weakness—it's strength. - Leaders live the standard. PPE worn right, lockout verified, briefings taken seriously. Crews notice.
-   Leaders make time for safety, even when production screams louder. That choice sets the tone.

Accountability is not about punishment, it's about ownership. Ownership says: "This is my standard. I don't delegate it. I don't excuse it. I live it."

A crew without accountability crumbles. A crew with it becomes resilient. Accountability is oxygen. Without it, the culture suffocates.

## Building Feedback on the Culture

Feedback isn't a quarterly review. It's a rhythm. It's the pulse of a crew that refuses to settle.

- Toolbox talks become two-way conversations, not scripts. Apprentices speak, veterans share, everyone learns.
- post-task reviews happen after critical work: what went right, what went wrong, what we change next time.
- Peer checks keep crews honest. Journeymen correct apprentices. Apprentices ask questions that keep journeymen sharp.

But feedback without follow-through is noise. Documentation makes lessons stick. A near miss remembered only in someone's head fades. A near miss written, shared, and reviewed becomes a shield for the next worker. Survival is not memory—it's a documented legacy.

Crews that talk survive. Crews that act on feedback thrive. Crews that stay silent stagnate—and stagnation kills.

## The Survival Mindset: Never Settle, Never Stagnate

Stagnation is the most dangerous hazard on any job site. You won't find it listed on an SDS or marked with caution tape, but it lurks everywhere. The moment a crew thinks, "We've got this down," they've already started slipping.

The survival mindset says: "We're never done."

- Crews sharpen skills relentlessly. Yesterday's knowledge is not enough for today's hazards.
- Leaders asked tougher questions, not easier ones. They probe for blind spots.
- Improvement becomes oxygen. Stop improving, and the culture suffocates.

This mindset builds resilience. It prepares crews for the unexpected. It ensures that today's apprentice will inherit more than tools—

they'll inherit survival habits. Improvement is not for you—it's for the one coming behind you.

Legacies aren't built by perfect jobs. They're built by crews that refused to stagnate. Never settle. Never coast. Never assume yesterday's survival guarantees today's.

Epilogue: Survival Through Relentless Improvement

Continuous improvement is the ground you stand on. Auditing is the mirror that tells you the truth. Together, they create the line between survivors and statistics.

Every adjustment, every audit, every feedback loop is another brick in the wall that separates your crew from disaster. Stop building that wall, and disaster will come. Guaranteed.

Survival is not given. It is earned—every shift, every decision, every correction.

So here's the truth: you cannot check the box and coast. You cannot assume yesterday's habits will cover today's risks. Improvement is never done. Auditing is never finished. Survival is never guaranteed.

The graveyards are full of workers who thought yesterday's system was good enough. Don't join them. Keep sharpening. Keep learning. Keep building. That's how you stay grounded for life.


Introduction: Survival Is a System, not a Fluke
Survival in the trades is not just about avoiding dangers it is about mastering it. Every job site is a battlefield, and every worker is a soldier in steel-toed boots. The ones who make it home aren't just lucky, they're prepared. They've trained their instincts, honed their awareness, and built a system that doesn't rely on chance. That system is forged through repetition, reflection, and relentless improvement. It's not just about surviving today—it's about being ready for tomorrow, and the day after that.

Continuous Improvement in the Trades

Improvement is the heartbeat of a crew that refuses to settle. It's not a one-time fix—it's a daily grind. It's the apprentice who asks questions until the answers become second nature. It's the journeyman who rewrites the JHA because the job changed halfway through. It's the foreman who pauses the crew to recalibrate, even when the clock is ticking. Improvement is not a luxury, it's a necessity. It's what separates the crews that thrive from the ones that just survive.

Auditing for Survival, Not Compliance
Auditing isn't about paperwork—it's about people. It's about walking around the site and seeing the truth behind the checklist. A survival audit doesn't just ask if the lockout tag is in place, it asks if the crew understands why it matters. It doesn't just verify PPE—it checks if the team respects the gear that protects them. Auditing is a conversation, not a confrontation. It's a chance to reinforce the culture, to build trust, and to ensure that the system is more than just words on a page.

Leadership and Accountability in Improvement
Leadership is the engine that drives improvement. It's the foreman who owns the mistake and turns it into a lesson. It's the superintendent who listens before he speaks. It's the journeyman who mentors the apprentice with patience and grit. Accountability isn't about blame, it's about ownership. It's about saying, "This is my crew, my standard, my responsibility." When leaders lead with integrity, crews follow with respect. And when accountability becomes the norm, improvement becomes unstoppable.

Building Feedback into the Culture
Feedback is the fuel of improvement. It's the toolbox talk that turns into a roundtable. It's the post-task review that uncovers the blind spot. It's the peer check that catches the mistake before it becomes a tragedy. Feedback must be constant, honest, and actionable. It must

be documented, shared, and revisited. A culture that embraces feedback is a culture that evolves. It's a crew that learns from every shift, every task, every challenge.

## The Survival Mindset: Never Settle, Never Stagnate

The survival mindset is a refusal to coast. It's the belief that good enough is never enough. It's the drive to sharpen skills, challenge assumptions, and push boundaries. It's the mindset that says, "We're not here to get by—we're here to get better." This mindset is contagious. It spreads from the foreman to the apprentice, from the veteran to the rookie. It becomes the foundation of a crew that doesn't just survive—they dominate.

## Epilogue: Survival Through Relentless Improvement

Survival is earned, not granted. It's built through every audit, every adjustment, every lesson learned. It's the legacy of crews who refused to settle, who chose to improve, who built systems that outlasted them. The graveyards are full of workers who thought they had figured it out. The survivors are the ones who knew they didn't—and kept learning anyway. Improvement is the path. Auditing is the mirror. Survival is the reward.

# Chapter 10

## Incident Investigations & Lessons Learned

# Chapter 10

## Introduction: Every Incident Is a Message

In the trades, incidents don't just happen, they speak. They're signals. Warnings. Lessons wrapped in pain. But too often, we treat them like isolated events. We clean up the mess, file the report, and move on. That mindset is dangerous.

Every incident is a message. And if we don't listen, we're setting ourselves up for repeat failure. This chapter is about how to investigate incidents with purpose, extract lessons that matter, and build a culture where learning from failure is part of survival.

When disaster or failure strikes—whether a near miss, an accident, or a profound mistake, it screams two things: you were vulnerable, and there's something to understand. That message might come wrapped in shame, in fear, in chaos. But it's there.

We often hush it, pretend nothing was wrong, blame someone, move on. But the truth is: every incident carries lessons—for the people involved, for leaders, for the chain of command, for the system.

To ignore it is to hand closure to ignorance. To face it is hard. But that's where change begins. Because the weight of what we don't address always shows up again, in one way or another.

---

## The Anatomy of an Incident Investigation

When something goes wrong in the field, whether it's a near miss, injury, or equipment failure, the clock starts ticking. The way you respond in the first few minutes sets the tone for everything that follows.

### Step 1: Secure the Scene

Before anything else, protect life and prevent further harm. Shut down equipment. Isolate energy sources. Administer first aid. Preserve the scene for investigation. This isn't just about compliance, it's about respect for the people involved.

The first hours. The first steps. Secure the people who are hurt. Secure the scene. Preventing more harm. Address urgent issues, medical, emotional, structural. If you don't contain it first, you'll be fighting the fire while trying to figure out how it started.

Step 2: Notify Leadership and Safety Personnel
Get the right people involved early. Supervisors, safety officers, and site managers need to be informed immediately. Delay leads to confusion, and confusion leads to missed details.

Step 3: Preserve Evidence
Don't clean up too fast. Document everything:

Photos of the scene

Equipment positions

PPE condition

Environmental factors

Evidence tells the story. If you erase it, you erase the truth.

Step 4: Interview Witnesses
Talk to everyone involved—quickly, calmly, and respectfully. Ask open-ended questions:

"What did you see?"

"What were you doing before the incident?"

"Did anything feel off?"

Avoid leading questions. Avoid blame. Just gather facts.

Step 5: Document Everything

Write it down. Record times, actions, statements, and observations.

Use standardized forms if available. The more thorough the documentation, the stronger the investigation.

Gather everything: facts, reports, interviews, photos, times, places. Speak to witnesses. Include those who made mistakes—because guilt doesn't cancel relevance. Don't accept assumptions, probe timelines, conflicting stories. Document both what people *say* and what evidence shows.

This anatomy is not academic. It's a blueprint for survival and integrity.

---

Root Cause vs. Surface Cause

Most investigations stop at the surface: "He didn't wear his gloves." "He didn't test the voltage." But those are symptoms—not causes. Real leadership digs deeper.

Surface Cause
This is what happened: PPE

wasn't worn

Lockout wasn't applied

Procedure wasn't followed

Important? Yes. But not enough.

Root Cause
This is why it happened:

Was the training inadequate?

Was the procedure unclear?

Was the schedule rushed?

Was the culture unsafe?

Tools like the 5 Whys, Fishbone Diagrams, and Taproot help uncover root causes. But the most powerful tool is mindset. Ask:

"What system allowed this?"

"What leadership failed to prevent this?"

"What warning signs were ignored?"

Root cause analysis isn't about blame—it's about building better systems.

Most of the damage after an incident comes from stopping at the surface. It's easy to blame the visible: a person's mistake, a broken tool, a missed step. But when you only treat those things, the wound returns.

When we dig root, we see how systems, culture, leadership, values, quiet tolerances set the stage.

The difference matters. Surface fixes are like patching a wall while ignoring the foundation is crumbling. Root fixes rebuilding the foundation.

---

## Leadership's Role in Investigations

When an incident occurs, leadership is on trial. Not in a courtroom—but in the eyes of the crew. How you respond determines whether trust is built or broken.

Lead with Integrity
Don't hide. Don't spin. Be transparent. "Here's what happened. Here's what we know. Here's what we're doing." That honesty builds credibility.

Create a No-Blame Culture

If people fear punishment, they'll hide the truth. Investigations must be about learning—not punishment. That doesn't mean ignoring accountability. It means separating intent from error.

Turning Investigations into Training
Every incident is a training opportunity. Use it to reinforce procedures, clarify expectations, and improve systems. Bring the crew together. Walk through the findings. Ask:

"What can we learn?"

"What will we change?" "How do

we prevent this again?"

Leadership turns pain into progress.

This is where the heart of any recovery lies. Leadership isn't just about giving orders—it's about owning truth, setting example, forging culture, taking responsibility—even for things that maybe weren't directly their fault. Real leadership shows when things go wrong.

Ownership and humility
A leader must say, "This happened on my watch." Even when they didn't cause it, they accept that the system under their care failed. That vulnerability earns trust. Blaming others, making excuses, or covering up only deepens wounds.

Setting environment for truth
Create spaces where people can speak up, even when their voice shakes. Encourage honest reporting, even near misses. Remove fear of reprisal. Make it clear: reporting isn't betrayal—it's service.

Providing resources & follow-through
Recommendations need support. Time, money, training, oversight. Leadership that asks for fixes but doesn't staff them, fund them, or monitor them fails. Change without resources is just gesture.

Leading by example

If leadership treats safety, accountability, truth as secondary—everyone else sees it. But if leadership shows up, investigates, learns, admits gaps, changes, that filters down. Culture shifts.

---

## Lessons Learned: Turning Pain into Protection

Lessons learned are the gold of every investigation. But too often, they're buried in reports and forgotten. Real leaders extract them, share them, and embed them into daily operations.

Document the Lesson Write
it clearly:

What happened

Why it happened

What was changed

Use plain language. Make it accessible. Don't bury it in jargon.

Share the Lesson
Lessons learned must be shared:

Toolbox talks

Safety briefings

Training sessions

Digital bulletins

Make it part of the culture. "Here's what happened last month. Here's what we learned. Here's what we're doing differently."

Embed the Lesson
Update procedures. Revise training. Adjust workflows. Lessons learned must lead to action. If nothing changes, the lesson is wasted.

When the dust settles, what must stay with us are the lessons. Lessons aren't just what *not to do again*, but what to *become*. Each incident should leave us clearer, stronger, more alert, more capable.

Sloppiness is often expensive. Minor neglect or "shortcuts" in protocol, training, inspection can brew disaster.

Communication gaps kill. What was assumed, what was left unsaid, what was vague are frequent culprits.

Culture is everything. A culture that tolerates near misses, that treats rules as burdens, or discourages speaking up, builds a graveyard of incidents.

Humans will err; systems must anticipate that. Redundancies, checks, backups, clear lines of accountability—not to punish, but to prevent cascading failures.

Healing must be holistic. Not just repairing what broke externally (machines, procedures), but what broke inside people: confidence, trust, safety, emotional stability.

These lessons are more than words on paper. They are guardrails for tomorrow.

---

The Survival Mindset: Fail Forward, Learn Fast

In Grounded for Life, survival isn't just about avoiding danger—it's about learning from it. Contractors who survive long-term aren't perfect. They make mistakes. They face incidents. But they learn fast. They fail forward.

Own Your Mistakes
Don't deflect. Don't deny. Own it. "I missed the lockout." "I rushed the test." That ownership builds respect—and it builds resilience.

Learn Loudly

Share what you learned. Help others avoid the same mistake. That's leadership. That's legacy.

## Protect the Next Generation

Every lesson learned is a gift to the next crew. The next apprentice. The next foreman. When you document, share, and embed lessons, you're protecting people you may never meet. That's what survival looks like.

When an incident happens, there are two paths: bitterness and blame, or renewal and empowerment. The survival mindset chooses the latter, even though it's harder.

## Resolve to see truth, even if it hurts

No whitewashing. No lying to self. You accept discomfort, you face the truth. Only that gives you power to change.

## Resilience, not denial

Resilience means you don't pretend nothing happened. You feel, you assess, you adapt. You carry scars—but don't let them define you.

## Learning as loyalty

When you learn from failure, you're honoring those who were hurt, preventing others from being hurt, fulfilling responsibility.

## Proactivity over passivity

Waiting for someone else to investigate, waiting for orders, waiting for crisis to pass—those are traps. A survival mindset pushes forward: asking questions, making small or big fixes, pressing for change.

## Compassion—for self, for others

Incidents hurt people. Emotions spill. Blame, guilt, shame all who show up. A survival mindset includes forgiveness, learning to care—for those who made mistakes, for those affected, and for yourself.

## Final Thoughts: Investigate to Elevate

Incident investigations aren't just about compliance. They're about culture. They're about leadership. They're about survival.

When something goes wrong, don't just fix the damage. Fix the system. Fix the mindset. Fix the future.

Because in this business, every incident is a message. And if you listen, you don't just survive—you elevate.

We are only as safe as what we refuse to overlook. Incidents aren't disruptions; they are teachers. The question isn't whether we'll have incidents, it's how we handle them when they come.

If we do this investigation with courage, leadership with humility, learning with purpose, survival with compassion, then incidents become turning points. They become the raw material from which safer, wiser, more humane systems are built.

Don't settle for Band Aids. Rebuild the foundation. Don't allow shame to hide truth. Let accountability become your compass

## Closing Reflection

### Closing Reflection: The Legacy We Leave Behind

Survival isn't just about making it through the day—it's about building something that lasts. Every decision we make, every correction we enforce, every lesson we pass down becomes part of a legacy that outlives us. The trades are unforgiving, but they're also noble. They demand grit, heart, and relentless discipline.

Leadership isn't a title, it's a responsibility. It's the quiet courage to speak up, the humility to admit mistakes, and the strength to hold the line when it matters most. Continuous improvement isn't a corporate slogan—it's the lifeblood of crews who refuse to settle. It's the difference between surviving and thriving.

So, here's the charge: Be the kind of leader who leaves the jobsite better than you found it. Be the kind of crew member who sharpens others by your example. Build systems that protect, habits that endure, and a culture that refuses to stagnate.

Because in the end, survival isn't just about today, it's about tomorrow. It's about the next apprentice who steps onto the site, the next foreman who takes the reins, the next generation who inherits our standards. Let them inherit strength. Let them inherit wisdom. Let them inherit a legacy built on relentless improvement.

Stay grounded. Stay sharp. Stay alive.

# Chapter 11

## Job Briefings & Pre-Task Planning

# Chapter 11

## Introduction: Planning Isn't Optional—It's Survival

In the trades, we don't get the luxury of "routine." Every job, every site, every crew is different. And every day brings a new set of risks. That's why job briefings and pre-task planning aren't just formalities, they're survival tools. They're the first line of defense against injury, chaos, and failure.

I've seen it too many times: a crew skips the briefing, rushes into work, and ends up in a situation they weren't prepared for. Sometimes it's a near miss. Sometimes it's a life-changing injury. And sometimes, it's a fatal mistake that could've been avoided with ten minutes of planning.

This chapter is about changing that mindset. It's about dealing with job briefings and pre-task planning with the seriousness they deserve. Because when you plan like your life depends on it—it usually doesn't have to. And in this line of work, that's the only bet worth taking.

## The Anatomy of a Solid Job Briefing

A job briefing isn't a speech. It isn't a chance for a supervisor to check a box. A briefing is a tactical conversation. It's where leadership meets accountability, and where every crew member gets aligned on the mission ahead.

OSHA 1910.269(c) requires that briefings cover hazards, work procedures, special precautions, energy source controls, and PPE. But real-world safety is never just about regulations it's about culture. A "compliant" briefing might cover the basics, but a committed briefing digs deeper:

- What exactly are we doing today?

- What could go wrong, and how do we stop it before it does?
- Who is doing what task, and do they have the training and equipment to do it safely?
- What's the plan if something changes—because something always changes?
- Who is in charge, and how will communication flow if the unexpected happens?

A good briefing has a leader, but not a dictator. The best ones are led by someone who knows both the work and the crew—not just someone with a title. When the briefing is interactive, when questions are encouraged and even pushed, people listen. If your crew isn't asking questions, that silence is dangerous. Silence means either they're confused or checked out. And both can kill.

Lesson learned: Treat briefings as conversations, not monologues. The more voices in the circle, the fewer sirens later in the day.

Pre-Task Planning: Real Work Starts Before the Work

Every great crew knows that the real work starts before the first tool is lifted. Pre-task planning is the foundation. It's where you build the blueprint for survival. It's where hazards are identified before they become incidents, and where roles and responsibilities are defined so that everyone knows their lane.

Hazard Identification
Tools like a Job Hazard Analysis (JHA) or a Field Level Risk Assessment (FLRA) aren't paperwork—they're weapons against complacency. When you stop and look around, you find more than just electrical hazards. You find fall risks where guardrails are missing, pinch points waiting to trap hands, environmental factors like extreme heat or storms rolling in. The most dangerous hazards are the ones no one names.

PPE & Equipment Checks

If you're putting gloves on, do you know if they're rated for the voltage you're about to face? Has the meter you're holding been calibrated and tested today, or are you trusting yesterday's assumptions? Is the lockout/tagout kit complete—or did someone walk off with the last lock? An arc flash suit sitting in a bag isn't a guarantee of safety unless it's been inspected and is in good condition. Gear is only lifesaving when it's ready.

Permits & Procedures
Every worksite has different requirements. Hot work permits. Confined space entry. Energized work protocols. Lockout/tagout documentation. These aren't red tape, they're shields. Each permit is a reminder that someone recognized the hazard before you walked into it blind. Skipping the permit step is skipping survival itself.

Crew Readiness
One of the most overlooked parts of planning is the crew itself. Who's standing in front of you today? Are they fit for duty? Did one guy fight with his wife last night and didn't sleep? Is another distracted by financial stress? Is someone hungover, or worse, under the influence? Fatigue, stress, and distraction are silent killers. Pretask planning is the only chance you have to catch them before they show up in the middle of a critical task.

Lesson learned: A job doesn't start with tools—it starts with people. If your people aren't ready, your plan doesn't matter.

Field-Level Risk Assessment: Dynamic Safety in Real Time

The field changes fast. Weather shifts. Equipment fails. The scope expands mid-job. That's why static planning isn't enough. You need dynamic risk assessment—the ability to evaluate and adapt in real time.

Field-Level Risk Assessment (FLRA) empowers crews to:
- Pause when conditions change.
- Reassess hazards with fresh eyes.

- Adjust procedures without shame.

- Communicate updates before the work resumes.

I've seen crews saved by what we in the Navy call an "operational pause." In construction, it's just smart work. If something feels off, stop. Debrief. Replan. Then proceed.

The most powerful thing a leader can say on a jobsite isn't "get it done." It's "stop—let's make sure." When workers know they're allowed to stop, they feel trusted. And when they feel trusted, they speak up. That's how you build a culture where people look out for one another instead of just for themselves.

Lesson learned: Real safety isn't static. It's alive. It moves with the crew, with the weather, with the job. The minute you lock it in stone, you've already lost.

Real-World Example: The Missed Briefing That Nearly Killed a Crew

A few years ago, I was called in to investigate an arc flash incident on a commercial jobsite. The crew had skipped the morning briefing because they were "behind schedule." They energized a panel without verifying the absence of voltage. The result? A flash that destroyed the equipment and caused a near miss that could have been a lot worse, and it shut down the site for weeks.

The root cause wasn't just a missed test, it was a missed conversation. No one asked, "Are we ready?" No one confirmed PPE. No one reviewed the procedure. They were in too much of a hurry to stop and align. That's the power of a job briefing. It's not about compliance—it's about catching the small things that can kill.

Lesson learned: A 10-minute briefing can prevent a six-month shutdown. Speed without clarity is nothing but chaos with a countdown clock.

Common Failures & How to Avoid Them

Most job briefings fail because they're rushed, vague, or ignored. Here are the failures I've seen repeatedly—and how to fix them:

- Skipped Briefings – Make them mandatory. No briefing, no work.
- One-Way Communication – If your briefing sounds like a lecture, it's not working. Ask questions. Demand answers. Pull your crew into the conversation.
- No Hazard Depth – Don't stop at "electrical hazard." Define the arc flash boundary. Explain the shock risk. Walk through mitigation. Specifics save lives.
- No Accountability – Assign roles. Who's the safety lead? Who's watching the lockout station? Who's responsible for rescue procedures?
- No Follow-Up – Briefings aren't one-and-done. Debrief after breaks, after scope changes, after near misses. Safety has to be refreshed, or it fades.

Lesson learned: If your crew isn't engaged, your plan isn't working. And if your plan isn't working, it's just a matter of time before the job site teaches you a lesson the hard way.

Leadership in Briefings: Setting the Tone

Leadership isn't about barking orders. It's about setting the tone. In job briefings, that means showing up prepared, speaking with clarity, listening with intent, and holding people accountable.

The truth is, crews mirror their leaders. If you're sloppy, they'll be sloppy. If you're sharp, they'll rise to the occasion. The job briefing is the first moment of the day where that tone is set.

Great leaders:
- Ask for input instead of pretending they have every answer.
- Encourage questions without rolling their eyes.
- Reinforce safety protocols by practicing them in plain view.
- Lead by example.

And they don't just talk safety—they live it. They wear their PPE correctly. They follow lockout/tagout steps. They stop working when needed, even if it means a delay. That's how you build trust. And trust is the foundation of every safe crew.

Lesson learned: The crew doesn't just follow the plan, they follow you. Show them what survival looks like.

The Mindset Shift: From Compliance to Commitment

Too many contractors treat job briefings like a compliance issue. Clipboards, checkboxes, and signatures. But the best crews treat them like commitment. A commitment to each other. A commitment to the mission. A commitment to going home safe at the end of the day.

This is where culture is born. Not just in policies, but in practices. Not just in rules, but in reasons. When safety becomes part of who you are, not just what you do, everything changes. Compliance will keep you legal. Commitment will keep you alive.

Lesson learned: Rules don't build culture. People do. Build a crew that doesn't just comply but commits.

Planning Is Protection: The Survival Mindset

Planning isn't paperwork. It's protection. It's how you survive the job, the week, and the career. Contractors who plan well don't just avoid injuries—they build reputations. They get rehired. They lead crews. They become the ones others look to when things get tough.

So here's the mindset shift:
• Don't treat briefings as routine. Treat them as critical.
• Don't rush planning. Invest in it.
• Don't assume safety. Confirm it.

In this business, you don't get second chances. You get one shot to plan right, lead right, and work right. Make it count.

Final lesson learned: The job briefing isn't just the start of the day. It's the start of survival.

One of the most powerful tools in a leader's arsenal is the ability to listen. During job briefings, listening isn't passive—it's active engagement. When a crew member raises a concern, that's not a disruption; it's a gift. It's a chance to catch something you might've missed. I've learned that the quietest guy on the crew often sees the most. Give him space to speak, and you might just avoid your next incident.

Another critical aspect of planning is understanding the environment. Are we working near live traffic? Is there wildlife in the area? Are we in a high-crime zone where tools might walk off if left unattended? These aren't just background details, they're operational factors. A good plan accounts for the job and the environment it lives in.

Documentation is another area where crews often fall short. A welldocumented briefing isn't just about covering your ass—it's about creating a record of intent. If something goes wrong, that document shows what was known, what was planned, and what was communicated. It's a snapshot of your mindset before work began. And in court—or in a hospital—that snapshot matters.

I also want to touch on the importance of mental health in planning. We talk about physical readiness, but what about emotional readiness? A crew member going through a divorce, grieving a loss, or battling depression is carrying a weight that affects focus and reaction time. Leaders need to be aware, not intrusive. A simple 'You good today?' can open a door that keeps someone safe.

Let's not forget the role of mentorship in job briefings. When a seasoned journeyman takes a moment to explain the 'why' behind a safety step to an apprentice, that's culture-building. That's how you pass down not just knowledge, but values. And those values are what keep the next generation alive.

Technology is also changing the game. Digital JHAs, mobile apps for hazard tracking, and real-time communication tools are making planning more dynamic. But tech is only as good as the people using it. Don't let a tablet replace a conversation. Use it to enhance the dialogue, not replace it.

Finally, I want to emphasize the importance of debriefing. At the end of the day, ask everyone: What went well? What didn't? What surprised us? This feedback loop is where real improvement happens. It's where tomorrow's plan gets better because of today's lessons.

Chapter 12

Leadership Under Voltage: Your Survival Standard

# Chapter 12

Every morning you walk on site, you're not just managing wires. You're walking among invisible threats. Voltage. Circuit parts. Energized conductors. Every connection, every panel, every splice—those are checkpoints. Misjudge one, slip once, and it isn't just your hand, it's worse.

This work demands a standard so strict it doesn't bend when someone says, "We'll be quick" or "Just this one time." You carry accountability in your bones—because in electrical construction, standard violations cost lives, not just fines.

Leadership here isn't about title. It's about enforcing what can't be compromised. Enforcing when no one else sees. Leadership is being the one who says, "Not yet," "No shortcut," "Wrong tool." That's your legacy.

## The Technical Backbone You Live By

To lead under voltage, you must carry knowledge. Not of theory, but of code. Legal minimums. What OSHA requires. What NFPA-70E demands. These aren't suggestions. They're the foundation under your boots.

### NFPA-70E: What It Demands

Electrically Safe Work Condition (ESWC) — An ESWC means everything: circuit parts de-energized, disconnected, locked/tagged, and tested. Until that's done, assume everything is live. NFPA-70E doesn't allow guessing. Electrical Safety Specialists+2EnSafe+2

Arc flash boundary & incident energy — Know them. Labels must show incident energy, hurled-back flash boundary. PPE must match risk. The tables in NFPA-70E, especially around arc flash hazard risk assessment and PPE categories, are your playbook. Electrical Safety Specialists+1

Qualified vs unqualified — You know who's supposed to do what. A "qualified person" under NFPA-70E is someone who has demonstrated skill, knowledge, training specific to that equipment or task. One person may be qualified for one panel but not qualified for another. No crossovers unless trained.

Training, retraining — Periodic refreshers are required. When job duties change. When new equipment is introduced. When incidents or near-misses happen. The standard demands you know the latest, not just "what we always did."

## OSHA 29 CFR Rules You Can't Ignore

29 CFR 1926 Subpart K (Electrical) Covers the installation of wiring, the safe design of electric equipment, safe work practices, environmental exposure, special equipment. In construction, you must comply. All temporary services, all circuits. No corners.

Lockout/Tagout — The part of the regulation that mandates: disconnect energy source, lock/tag it out, test to verify absence of voltage, protect against re-energization. Doesn't matter if you think it's low risk. If you're touching live parts or parts that may become energized, you follow the process.

Cable & cord safety — Frayed cords, damaged insulation, improper connections—OSHA demands you maintain tools and cords. If the insulation is compromised, you stop using it, tag it out. No workaround.

## How Real Leadership Works Under Voltage

You can know code. But if you don't live it, it doesn't matter. Real leadership enforces, every shift, every task. Not because you're paranoid—but because you respect the work, the risk, the human bodies involved.

## Rituals You Build That Save Flesh

### Shift-Start Hazard & Circuit Briefing

You gather your crew. You go over what circuits are energized or will be energized, what might introduce unexpected voltage, what panels need testing, who's touching what. You map out exposed live parts, what PPE is needed. You confirm who's qualified for what. This is every shift. No exceptions.

### Tool & Equipment Pre-check

Gloves, insulating tools, testers, meters, boots, arc-rated clothing. If something is shot—gloves cracked, meter leads frayed, boot soles torn—you remove it. Don't let someone work with faulty gear. That's not laziness; it's deadly.

### Lockout/Tagout and Testing

Before any work on circuits that could be energized, you disconnect, you lock, you tag, and you test. And if stored energy or capacitors exist, you discharge them. Only after that do you allow work. If you cannot establish an ESWC, you don't do energized work. Period.

### Arc Flash Boundaries & PPE Enforcement

The arc flash boundary is not optional. If it's defined, it's respected. If a task is within that boundary, even for a second, proper PPE must be on. Face shields, gloves, arc-rated clothing, whatever the standard tables require. No trade-offs.


## Communication & Tone: What Holds Under Pressure

When someone suggests a shortcut ("We don't have time," "Just this little bit"), you call it out—not angrily, but firmly. You ask "Which standard are we breaking here? What risk are you introducing?" You don't let morale or schedule override safety.

When someone makes a safety call or points out a hazard, you don't brush them off. You acknowledge. You fix. You reinforce and investigate the potential harm. That builds trust.

Under emergencies—surges, unexpected energization, wet conditions—you stay grounded. Clear. Direct. Rehearsed responses. Stop working if something feels unsafe. Measure twice. Act once.

## Common Failures That Destroy Trust & Cost Lives

These are the things that leaders rationalize. They always start small. If you don't snuff them out, they grow.

Assuming de-energized means safe, without verifying — "We shut off the breaker" doesn't cut it. You must test. Voltage can back feed. Capacitors can hold. Without testing, you're gambling.

Low Voltage = Low Risk — Nothing could be further from the truth. Many arc flash and shock injuries happen in "low voltage" systems. If voltage is above 50 V in many jurisdictions, or any energized parts, the standard kicks in. PPE, boundaries, everything. You don't dismiss risk simply because it feels small.

Damaged gear tolerated — Gloves with tiny cuts. Meter leads slightly frayed. Boots are a little worn. Tools missing insulation. If you allow that, you're asking for failure. Every piece of gear you trust must be intact.

Inconsistency in enforcement — If you enforce lockout/tagout sometimes, slip sometimes; if you demand PPE when supervisors are around, but allow it slack when they're not—that cynicism builds. People stop believing. Standards fall away.

Favoring speed over safety — Production demands, tight deadlines. You hear "we'll just do this part live," "we'll turn panels on early," "don't wait for X." That is the bending point. Every time you let speed over safety, you're seed-planting future hazard.

## Survival Mindset: How You Think When Pressure Rises

You don't just train for normal. You lead for when things go sideways. That mindset distinguishes who walks away unscathed from who doesn't.

You assume hazard until you have proven safe. Even when job's done a thousand times, ground is wet, conditions dusty, wires exposed, circuits unidentified—hazard lives.

You plan for emergencies: know your escape routes, shut-offs, PPE stash points, test tools stored, gloves accessible, arc-flash suits reachable. Not after accident—before.

You accept no partial compliance. Pack the right PPE before going up. Test before touching. Respect boundaries always. Even when nobody else notices.

You lead by doing. Show up early. Inspect PPE. Run the walkthrough. Listen to concerns. When you do, your crew sees the standard is real—not just talk.

What You Own, Right Now

Here's a list: what you must start doing today, what you must insist on, what you must teach. This is your survival checklist.

Mandatory Live Work Assessment
For any live or potentially live work, you do an assessment: is this energized work justified? Can the circuit be de-energized? Can you establish an ESWC? Do you have the correct PPE and tools?

PPE Audit Before Shift
Walk among your crew. Look at gloves, boots, clothing, tool insulation, testers. Remove everything unsafe.

Boundary Labels & Zones
All panels, all boxes, all equipment must be labeled for arc flash boundary and incident energy. Assign and mark restricted approach boundaries clearly.

### Verified Lockout/Tagout Process

Don't accept "I turned it off." You want locks on. Tags visible. Test results recorded. Any capacitors discharged. All parts are safe.

### Electrical Safety Training & Patrols

Regular refreshers on what's changed in NFPA-70E latest edition. Walk around the site randomly. Watch for boundary violations, nonqualified people near live parts, gear misuse. Corrections come immediately.

### Stop Work Authority for Everybody

If any person sees or feels something unsafe, they stop work. Full stop. No judgment. Then you reset. Then you move forward when truly safe.

### Lead the Morning Briefing with Standards

Every morning: identify possible energized circuits, note environmental risks (rain, damp surfaces, weather), clarify who's qualified. Make the standard the starting line—when you skip that, you start on dangerous ground.


### Final Word: What It Costs If You Don't

You already know. One misfire. One bad splice. One misjudged live panel. One frayed insulation. One inappropriate tool.

What happens if you don't enforce?

Injury. Burn. Electrocution. Permanent damage. Maybe worse.

Trust erodes. Crew starts doing what they see, not what they're told. Standards become suggestions. Safety becomes a memory.

Legal trouble. Fines. Shutdowns. Liabilities. Workers comp nightmares.

What happens if you do enforce?

You build a crew that looks out for each other. That refuses shortcuts. That checks gear. That demands PPE. That leads in risky moments.

You build credibility. People believe you when you say, "not yet." They know you mean every word.

You leave something behind. Not just completed panels—but culture. Safety. Respect. Legacy.

If this chapter moves from words into actions, it changes more than day's output. It changes what people expect at your site. It changes what you teach. What unqualified notice. What gets fixed. What gets cut.

Keep the standard. Live it. Enforce it. Because under voltage, your voice can make the difference between walking away whole—or not walking away at all.

Leadership in Electrical Construction: Survival Guide Mentality

You are working with energy. You are fighting gravity, voltage, deadlines, wet ground, overhead hazards. One slip, one oversight, one assumption—it can cost more than a paycheck. It can cost lives. In electrical construction, leadership isn't just a standard. It's what keeps you alive. Every decision, every tool, every second matters.

You lead by standards so rigid they don't bend under pressure. You own accountability like its oxygen—because here, without it, you choke.

The Field Leader's Role When Wires & Voltage Are in the Mix

You're more than supervisor. You are the gatekeeper of safety between energized circuits and living flesh. You set the atmosphere where live power becomes respected, not abused, where the crew does not gamble with shortcuts. In electrical construction, you carry the responsibility for every connection you make, for every live source you touch.

Leading by Example

Wear arc flash PPE properly—not just when inspectors are watching. Helmets, gloves, face shields, insulated tools. If you don't walk that talk, you've lost your voice.

Follow Lockout/Tagout every time. De-energize first. Test for dead. Ground if required. Then I begin work. There is no compromise.

Use correct tools. If a tester is scratched, a meter is compromised, a cord is frayed trash it or tag it out. Quality matters. The tool is part of the standard.

Consistency Builds Trust

If you say you'll test circuits before touching them, do it every time. No exceptions.

If safe distances from overhead or underground power lines are part of planning .

If weather turns wet, if the insulation gets wet, if there's moisture where it shouldn't be, don't carry on because it's inconvenient. You stop. You mitigate. Crew trusts a leader who honors their body's fragility.

Enforcing Standards Without Ego (Wires Do Not Care Who's Ruling)

When someone bypasses a GFCI or ground fault protection because "we'll be quick"—you stop that.

When someone plugs in tools with damaged insulation "just for now"—you cut that off.

A correction isn't a lecture. It's a reminder that electricity is unforgiving. That standard isn't about you looking good, it's about everyone walking home.

## Accountability Systems That Actually Work in Electrical Trades

When the risk includes live voltage, fire, arcs, and the possibility of burns or worse, your accountability systems need to be iron-clad.

### Morning Rituals & Safety Audits, Electrical Style

Start every shift with a live-work briefing. Identify which circuits will be energized. Clarify who's worked what. Double check who's qualified.

Use formal hazard assessments focused on electrical risk: overhead/underground lines, condition of wiring, insulation, moisture, tool status.

Walk-throughs aren't optional. Inspect panels, verify lockout/tagout zones are respected, check tool integrity, cord integrity, look for stray wires.

### Peer Checks & Crew Feedback

Encourage peers to watch each other's backs. A second set of eyes on circuits before energizing can mean difference between safety and disaster.

Feedback should be grain-of-sand early—not after an incident. When someone sees a frayed cord, call it out. When someone notices a panel cover loose, flag it. Reward the awareness.

### Correcting Without Conflict (When Voltage is Your Adversary)

Pull someone aside if they're about to violate a standard. Not shame but to protect.

Ask "what made you think this was acceptable?" Listen. Find gaps. Repair behavior. Don't turn it into a shouting match. You want compliance, not resentment.

Never let a small shortcut become precedent. Voltage doesn't respect precedent—it respects physics and safety boundaries.

Ownership vs Blame

When something fails—when a circuit faults, when an arc flash event almost happens—don't ask "who messed up," ask "what system failed, what decision was missed, and how do we fix it as a crew."

When you, as leader, missed something—own it. "I should have caught that weak insulation." That pulls people in. That underwrites trust.

Use near-misses as lessons. Use them so people don't hide, but so they see value in reporting before damage happens.

Leading Under Pressure — Electrical Edition

When the clock is tight. When power needs to be turned on "today." When rain is creeping in. When circuits aren't behaving. That's when leadership is tested.

Decision-Making in High-Risk Moments

If there's any doubt that a source is de-energized—do not energize. Stop. Verify. Use proper testers. If something doesn't look right—back off.

Know your safe approach distances. Understand Arc flash ratings. If exposure calculations show danger—redesign the task, get better PPE, or delay until safe.

Use stop-work authority broadly. You, or any competent crew member, must be able to halt work if safety is in doubt.

Staying Calm When Circuits Snap

When a flash, surge, unexpected voltage spike happens—you respond, not react. Breathing, clear commands, problem isolation.

Maintain communication. "I need everyone clear of that panel." "Cut power upstream." "Switch back once safe."

Emotion under control is what gives space for action. Panic kills precision. In electrical work, precision saves.

Communication & Emotional Control

Use simple, exact instructions: which phase, which neutral, which grounding. Miscommunication kills.

Speak about the risk. Don't mince words about what could happen. Dismissals or jokes about "light shock" erode seriousness.

Control tone. A sharp calm tone demands attention better than a shout does. Respect gives you response.

Developing Leaders: Electrical Crews

Your legacy is not just in your work—it's in the people you raise who keep standard alive.

Mentorship & Passing the Torch

Identify those who respect electricity—not just respect it but fear it enough to treat it right. Those who ask questions about safety rather than how fast.

Give them responsibility: inspect for insulation integrity, lead lockout/tagout audits, oversee PPE checking. Let them teach small segments. Let them grow.

Spotting Potential Under Voltage

Someone who pulls you aside to say, "I saw something wrong" rather than keep quiet. Someone who declines shortcut offers. Someone who speaks up about tool defects. That's potential.

Their eyes are already seeing what you want them to see. Pull them forward.

## Training vs Testing

More than classroom or code. Simulated conditions. Power down work. Live work where allowed—but tested, safe, supervised. Mistakes in simulation are cheaper than in real life.

Run drills: what if the GFCI fails, what if insulation gets wet, what if a cable is accidentally energized. Let leaders practice responses. Reflect after. That builds muscle memory.

# Common Failures & Fatal Flaws in Electrical Field Leadership

You will face breakdowns. Recognizing them early saves more than reputation; it can save flesh.

## Giving In to Shortcut Temptations

"Just this panel"; "just this wire"; "just this day." Every "just this" chips away at standard.

When schedule pressure pushes corners—resist. Pressure is always the test. How you handle that test defines everything.

## Tool & Equipment Neglect

Damaged insulation, frayed cords, missing ground prongs. If you allow decent tools to degrade, you are inviting disaster.

Regular inspections and maintenance are not overhead, they are lifelines.

## Inconsistent Enforcement

If sometimes you force lockout/tagout and sometimes you let it slide—people learn what you tolerate.

Inconsistency kills credibility. Credibility is what gives your directives weight when it matters.

## Underestimating the Invisible Hazards

Moisture, overhead lines, underground utilities, induced voltage, backfeed. The hazards you can't see are the ones that kill unawares.

Always assume unseen risk until proven otherwise. That assumption should guide every action.

## Survival Mindset: Electrical Trade Version

These aren't motivational clichés. These are survival tools when voltage is your opponent, and the field is your battleground.

### Discipline

Electricians can't afford "good enough." Every spice is properly insulated. Every ground properly bonded. Every conductor routed cleanly.

Discipline means doing prep work: isolating, testing, grounding—before you ever touch a live feed.

Discipline means resisting complacency. Even after a thousand loadouts, a thousand safe days, there is always something that can go wrong.

### Humility

Electricity doesn't respect titles or ego. It strikes the ignorant and the arrogant first.

Lead by admitting you don't know every code nuance. Ask when uncertain. Be willing to stop and double-check under load.

Humility opens you to learning new standards, new tools, new techniques. It keeps you alive.

Grit

The hours will be long. The conditions will be bad. The job will come at weird hours. Sometimes in storms, in dark, in mud, in cold.

Grit means putting grit in your boots and still showing up. It means chasing perfection in execution even when everything else is hard.

You survive by staying longer in the arena than your doubts. By pushing through risk where others walk away—not recklessly, but intelligently.

Tactical Electrical Survival Moves You Can Use Right Now

To anchor this in action, here are specific moves you can own, today, to make your leadership and your crew safer, sharper.

Circuit Verification Ritual — Before work begins on any circuit, verify de-energization with two independent testers. If possible, ground it. Mark locks/tags visibly.

Insulation Integrity Check — Set a standard: cords, gloves, tools inspected at start of shift. Any damage = removed. Never used.

Live Source Awareness Mapping — Map out overhead and buried lines, live panels, and post warning boundaries. Communicate with all crews. Mark them physically.

Weather Stop Rule — Establish conditions under which you stop work involving live circuits (rain, moisture, lightning). Enforce without exception.

Small Group PPE Enforcement — Assign "PPE guardians" on crew: one or more people responsible each shift to audit PPE compliance (gloves, face shield, flame resist, etc.). Call out lapses.

Mock Emergency Drill — Run a quick simulation (maybe 5-10 min) of an electrical emergency: e.g. unexpected energization, arc fault event. Practice shutdown, response, accountability communication.

"Stop & Reflect" Moments — After a critical action (energizing, tying in a big load, cutting into panels), pause. Ask: what did we do well? What could kill us that we missed? What's the margin of error here?

Delegate Audits — Rotate responsibility: one crew member assesses the state of tools, groundings, and insulation. Another checks live sources. Let ownership spread.


Final Thought: Why This Standard Matters More Than You Think

Because in electrical trade work, you don't just lead tasks. You lead decisions that decide which circuits are safe, which panels live, which wires are energized. One misstep isn't just a "delay" — it can be trauma. It changes lives.

Leadership with accountability isn't optional, it's your shield. If you live that standard, you become more than a foreman, supervisor, or electrician. You become the reason people trust the wires, the tools, the job site, the system. You become the reason someone walks home whole at the end of the day.

You lead with clarity. With discipline. With respect for the invisible. That is leadership under voltage.

# Chapter 13

## Cost of complacency

# Chapter 13

Complacency is a silent killer on the job site. It doesn't show up with flashing lights or loud

alarms creep in slowly, disguised as routine. You've done the task a hundred times,

maybe a thousand. You stop double-checking your gear. You skip the tailgate talk. You assume the other guy saw the hazard. That's when it strikes.

Real-world example? A journeyman electrician in Texas was installing conduit in a familiar substation. He'd done it for years. But this time, he didn't test the voltage — he assumed the line was dead.
It wasn't. He survived, but with burns and permanent nerve damage. All because he got comfortable.

Complacency often hides behind confidence. You think you've got it handled. You've seen worse. You've worked in tougher conditions. But the job doesn't care how experienced you are it only takes one slip.

Psychological traps feed complacency. Familiarity breeds shortcuts. Repetition dulls awareness. You stop scanning the site like you used to. You stop asking questions. You stop listening to that gut feeling that says, Hold up — something's off. And Subtle signs of complacency? Watch for these: skipping PPE and ignoring a checklist, rushing through a lockout-tagout, assuming someone else handled the hazard.

These aren't mistakes — they're symptoms of a mindset that's drifting into danger. Crews that joke about safety rules, supervisors who roll their eyes at paperwork, or veterans who say I've been doing this for 30 years. Those are red flags. Complacency isn't just personal; it's cultural. And if you don't fight it, it spreads.

The antidote? Relentless awareness. Treat every job like it's your first day. Ask questions. Slow down. Double-check. Build habits that override comfort. Because the moment you stop respecting the risk is the moment it bites back.

Complacency doesn't matter how many years you've been in the trade. It doesn't matter how many certifications you've got. It waits for you to relax — then it hits. Stay sharp. Stay alive.

Complacency Creeping In

Complacency doesn't show up with a warning label. It creeps in when the job starts feeling routine. You've done it a hundred times, so you stop double-checking. You skip the meter check because the panel should be dead. You leave your gloves in the truck because you're just checking something real quick. That's how it starts. Not with a bang, but with a shrug.

It's the quiet killer. It hides behind phrases like we've always done it this way and nothing ever happened before; It convinces seasoned pros they're invincible and rookies that they're safe just because they're surrounded by experience. But electricity doesn't matter how long you've been in the trade. It doesn't matter if it's your first day or your thousandth. It Only cares if you respect it.

Every time you ignore a near miss, every time you let a shortcut slide, complacency gets stronger. It's not a one-time mistake, it's a pattern. And when that pattern becomes culture, you're not just risking gear—you're risking lives. Lives of people who trusted the system, trusted the crew, and trusted that someone was watching their back.

Culture

Culture isn't what's written in the safety manual—it's what happens when no one's watching. If your crew sees shortcuts rewarded and safety ignored, that's the culture. If the loudest voice on the job is the one saying just get it done,; that's the culture. And if complacency is tolerated, it becomes contagious.

You build culture one decision at a time. It starts with the little things—wearing your PPE even when it's uncomfortable, doing the job briefing even when you're behind schedule, calling out unsafe behavior even when it's your buddy. Those moments set the tone. They tell the crew what matters and what doesn't.

A strong safety culture doesn't happen by accident. It's built by leaders who walk the walk and crews who hold each other accountable. It's reinforced by systems that make safety the default, not the exception. And it's protected by people who refuse to let complacency take root. Because once it does, it spreads fast—and it's damn hard to kill.

Accountability

Accountability is the antidote to complacency. It's what keeps the crew sharp and the jobsite honest. Without it, bad habits go unchecked and near misses get buried. With it, every incident becomes a lesson, and every mistake becomes a warning. Job briefings, peer checks, near-miss reports, these aren't paperwork exercises. They're

survival tools. They force the conversation. They make you think. They shine a light on the corners where complacency hides. But tools are only as strong as the people who use them. If leaders don't demand accountability, it dies. If crews don't embrace it, it fades. And if the system doesn't support it, it fails.

Accountability means owning your role in safety. It means speaking up when something's off. It means documenting the close calls and learning from them. And it means never letting complacency slide—not once, not ever.

The survival mindset is what separates the discipline from the danger. It's the voice in your head that says check it again. It's the habit that makes you test every circuit, inspect every glove, and follow every procedure—every time.

In the electrical world, there are no second chances. Voltage doesn't care about your intentions. Arc flash doesn't care about your experience. And physics doesn't care about your excuses. The only thing that matters is respect. Respect for energy. Respect for the process. Respect for the risk.

The survival mindset means treating every task like its life or death—because sometimes, it is. It means refusing to let routines dull your awareness. It means training your crew to see danger even when it's quiet. And it means never letting your guard down, no matter how many times you've done the job.

Discipline is survival. Complacency is surrender. And in this trade, surrender isn't an option. So build the mindset. Live the mindset. And make damn sure your crew does too.

Survival Mindset

This isn't just a catchy phrase — it's the difference between going home or going to the hospital. A survival mindset means you walk onto every jobsite with your senses sharp, your awareness high, and your ego checked at the gate. You don't assume anything. You verify. You don't trust that panel is dead — you test it. You don't skip PPE because "it's just a quick task." You suit up like your life depends on it — because it does.

Real survival mindset means you're not just thinking about yourself. You're scanning the crew. You're watching for signs of fatigue, distraction, or shortcuts. You're the guy who speaks up when something feels off. You're the one who says, "Hold up — let's double-check that." That's leadership in the trenches.

You build this mindset through repetition, training, and storytelling. Share the close calls. Talk about the guy who got lit up because he didn't lock out. Remind the crew that every task has risks, even the ones we've done a thousand times. Survival mindset isn't fear it's respect. Respect for voltage, respect for procedure, and respect for the fact that one mistake can change everything.

Train your crew to think like survivors. Run drills. Ask "what if" questions. Make safety meetings real — not just checkbox sessions. When you build a crew that thinks like survivors, you build a crew that lasts.

Complacency Reminder

Complacency doesn't just show up with a red flag—it creeps in wearing your crew's uniform. It looks like routine. It sounds like we've done this a thousand times It hides behind phrases like we know what we're doing. But here's the truth: complacency kills. It's the silent partner in every near miss, every shortcut, every overlook hazard. It's the reason a seasoned operator forgets to lock out a panel. It's why a foreman skips the tailgate talk because everyone knows the drill and it's why a crew member ends up in the ER because no one double-checked the confined space monitor. Realworld consequences aren't theoretical. They're names on incident reports. Their families getting phone calls.

Their careers cut short. If you think it won't happen to you, you're already in danger. Stay sharp. Stay humble. Stay alive.

Call to Action

This isn't just another chapter—it's a wake-up call. If you're leading a crew, walking a site, or signing off on a JSA, you're holding lives in your hands. So, lead like it matters. Speak up when something feels off. Shut down the job if safety's compromised. Build a culture where vigilance is the norm, not the exception. Complacency is the enemy, and survival is the mission. From this moment forward, commit to being the one who sees the hazard before it strikes, who speaks up before silence costs a life, and who leads with grit, integrity, and urgency. Your crew is watching. Your legacy is forming. Make it count.

# Chapter 14

Inside the Flash

Chapter 14

In the trades, there are mistakes you can walk away from and mistakes you'll carry for life. But then there's the one mistake you might not walk away from at all: an arc flash.

People talk about arc flashes like they're just another line in the safety book. But the men and women who've stood inside one don't talk about it like that. They talk about the sound—the cannon-blast that shakes your chest. They talk about the light, the white-blue glare that blinds you before you even know what happened. They talk about the heat, the kind that doesn't just burn skin, but melts tools, clothes, and steel.

Arc flash is survival stripped down to milliseconds. It's not a theory. It's not a classroom slide. It's the kind of event that rewrites your life in less time than it takes to blink.

Survivors often describe how the world changes instantly. Before the flash, there's noise—machines humming, voices, tools clanging. After the flash, there's silence, broken only by screams or the hiss of fire. Some describe it as if time is split in two: the life they lived before and the one they were left with after.

This chapter isn't about scaring you. It's about telling the truth. Because inside the flash, there's no second chance, no curtain call, and no time to improvise. What you carry into that moment is all you have—and it will decide if you walk out at all.

Arc flash is what happens when electricity leaves the path it's supposed to follow and finds its own way through air. That air becomes plasma—hotter than the surface of the sun. We're talking thousands of degrees Fahrenheit in an instant (NFPA 70E, 2024).

That heat isn't alone. The energy expands violently, blasting pressure like a small bomb. It can turn tools into shrapnel. Panels blow open.

Steel bends. The sound is deafening, often measured over 140 decibels—loud enough to rupture eardrums (IEEE 1584).

And then there's the light. Not just brightness, but a superheated flash that can cause temporary or permanent blindness.

What's happening in that split-second is physics pushed to extremes. Copper vaporizes into plasma, expanding 67,000 times its original volume. Air ionizes, turning into a conductive path that feeds the arc. The fault energy cascades, multiplying as breakers, fail to open fast enough. It's not just a spark, it's a chain reaction of energy release.

Imagine standing in front of a furnace door the size of a car hood, and someone rips it open without warning. That's the intensity crews face when the arc erupts. And unlike fire, it doesn't spread slowly. It detonates instantly, leaving no margin for hesitation. Safety manuals call it "an arcing fault." Survivors call it hell in an instant.

What happens inside that flash? Violence—pure and simple.

First comes the light, blinding and white-hot. Then the heat hits. At two feet from the source, skin can suffer third-degree burns in under a tenth of a second. PPE buys time, but nothing stops the laws of physics.

The blast force follows. Workers have been knocked off ladders, thrown across switchgear rooms, slammed into concrete walls. Metal doors fly open like grenades. Bolts and screws become projectiles.

The violence doesn't stop at burns. Survivors report broken bones, concussions, puncture wounds from shrapnel, and collapsed lungs from blast pressure. Some don't even remember being thrown—they wake up on the ground, disoriented, with their tools melted into the floor.

The smell is unforgettable: burning insulation, scorched clothing, vaporized copper. It lingers in the nose, long after the incident is over.

Crews describe it as the smell of fear, because it marks the moment everything changed.

The human body isn't built to process events this fast. By the time your brain registers danger, the arc has already done its damage. That's why discipline before the flash is the only thing that matters. Inside the event, there's nothing left to do but endure.

The Electrical Safety Foundation International (ESFI) estimates that over 30,000 arc flash incidents occur annually in the U.S. (ESFI). Many don't make the news because they're "non-fatal." But non-fatal doesn't mean non-life changing.

A journeyman in Texas survived an arc flash at 480 volts. His gloves and shirt ignited. He spent six weeks in a burn unit, endured skin grafts on both arms, and lost partial use of his left hand. He lived—but every shower for the rest of his life would remind him of that day.

Another case reported by NIOSH: an electrician was troubleshooting a 13.8 kV breaker without verifying absence of voltage. The arc vaporized copper bus bars and blew him ten feet back. He survived only because of distance—but his hearing never returned (NIOSH, 2015).

Arc flash scars aren't just physical. Survivors talk about the smell of their own burning clothes, the panic of trying to breathe through smoke, the way their crew looked at them afterward. The mental toll is permanent. Some never step into another electrical room again.

Families pay the price too. Children watch their parents live with scars, pain, and surgeries. Spouses become caregivers. Careers end overnight, not because of lack of skill, but because one arc flash rewrote the future. Survivors often say the scars remind them every day that survival isn't luck—it's preparation.

Luck is the most dangerous myth in this trade.

"I've been doing it this way for 20 years."
"I just need to get this breaker reset."
"It only takes a second."

That's the language of luck. And luck runs out fast.

Arc flash doesn't care about your years of experience. It doesn't matter if you're the fastest hand on the crew. It doesn't matter if the job is behind schedule. All it takes is one slip of a tool, one mislabeled breaker, one skipped test-before-touch.

The gambler's mindset is deadly. Doing something unsafe repeatedly without consequence convinces workers that it's safe. That's how complacency grows—not from ignorance, but from routine. But statistics prove otherwise: the majority of arc flash victims aren't rookies. They're mid-career workers, the very people who "knew better" but trusted luck one too many times.

The idea that "it hasn't happened yet, so it won't happen" is poison. That's not safe, it's gambling. And the odds always catch up.

OSHA has made it clear: workers must be protected from arc flash hazards through PPE, boundaries, and safe work practices (OSHA 1910.333). NFPA 70E reinforces it: verify absence of voltage every time. The rules aren't written because someone was lucky. They're written because thousands weren't.

Survival doesn't start when the flash erupts. By then, it's already too late. Survival starts with preparation.

- PPE Selection: Arc-rated clothing, face shields, balaclavas, gloves, and suits exist for a reason. A 40 cal suit looks overkill—until you're in a room that just turned into a furnace. For certain high-energy tasks, a 100 cal suit is required. It's heavy, hot, and uncomfortable— but it gives you those life-saving seconds.

-   Test Before Touch: This is the creed. NFPA 70E doesn't say "trust the breaker." It says verify absence of voltage. That means meters, probes, and confirming every single time.

-   Energized Work Permits: If the job requires working near or on energized equipment, the standard demands a written permit, justification, and documented risk controls. That paperwork isn't a prop—it's a survival script when done right.

-   Boundaries and Distance: Shock boundaries, arc flash boundaries—these aren't abstract numbers. They're the invisible blast radius. Respecting them is the difference between getting singed and getting killed.

Preparation looks slow. Preparation looks stubborn. But preparation is survival.

The reality is, crews often resist PPE because of discomfort. Suits fog up, restrict movement, and feel unbearable in the summer. But every survivor who walked away from a flash in PPE will tell you: the inconvenience is nothing compared to the pain of third-degree burns. Preparation is more than compliance—it's respect for your own life and the lives of your crew.

Arc flash survival isn't just about the individual. It's about leadership. A foreman who lets the crew work live because "it's faster" is gambling with lives. A safety manager who praises zero incidents while ignoring mislabeled switchgear is setting the stage for tragedy.

Leadership means saying no when everyone else wants yes. It means burning schedule time to verify, suit up, and reset barricades. It means backing the apprentice who refuses to enter the panel until the test meter says zero.

Good leaders don't just manage, they take responsibility. They don't watch the play from the office seats. They step into the blast zone with their crews and set the standard by example.

History is full of examples where leadership saved lives. Crews tell stories of foremen who shut down jobs despite pressure, who refused shortcuts, and who insisted on PPE. Those leaders may have been unpopular in the moment, but when the flash erupted—or when it didn't—it was their discipline that made the difference. In contrast, failed leadership is written in injury reports, obituaries, and court cases. The difference is always the same: who valued survival more, the schedule or the crew?

Arc flash is where the theater ends. Props don't help. Banners don't burn any more slowly. Zero-incident dashboards don't put skin back on hands.

Survival isn't about pretending. It isn't about optics. It's about standards. The standard to test every circuit. The standard to wear gear every time. The standard to shut it down when your gut says no.

This is the line between acting and living. Between playing the part and making it home.
When the flash erupts, you either built your survival standard ahead of time—or you didn't. And there's no rewinding that tape.

Theater celebrates appearance. Survival demands principle. The two will never meet. If your standard is grounded in truth, you'll never need a stage to prove it. If your standard is built on shortcuts, the flash will expose it instantly. This is why survival isn't a show, it's a standard lived in every decision, every test, every lockout, every suitup. Your crew doesn't need an actor. They need someone grounded in survival, not performance.

Arc flash isn't dramatic, it's deliberate. It punishes shortcuts instantly and rewards discipline quietly.
The men and women who survive don't walk out because they were lucky. They walk out because they were prepared. Because they tested. Because they wore gear. Because they refused to play along in the theater of shortcuts.

This chapter is your reminder: the flash will never give you a warning, but it always gives you a choice—before it happens. Your standard is that choice.
Carry it, live it, enforce it. Because inside the flash, there are no scripts, no props, and no curtain calls. Only survival.

And when you walk out—scarred, sweating, or shaken—you prove something bigger than luck. You prove that survival is deliberate. That's the legacy you carry into the next shift, and the lesson you leave for the apprentice watching. This isn't theater. This is life. And you only get one performance.

# Chapter 15

The calls nobody wants to make

## Introduction – The Phone That Burns in Your Hand

If you've been in the trades long enough, you've seen your share of close calls. Tools dropped, sparks flying, guys walking away shaking their heads. You've seen the ambulance come through the gate and the crew go silent. But there's something worse. Something no one warns you about. The moment you realize you must pick up the phone.

Not to call the power company. Not to call the office. To call home. Nobody prepares you for that. There's no OSHA standard with a script. NFPA 70E won't tell you what to say. Yet it's as real a hazard as the breaker you're standing in front of. If you're a foreman, a supervisor, a safety lead — that phone could end up in your hand. And when it does, it weighs more than steel. That phone carries death. And when you speak into it, you deliver it.

## The Moment Before the Call

After an accident, the sirens take the noise with them. The gate shuts, and everything feels wrong. Tools are still lying in the mud. A pair of gloves is still by the panel; fingers curled like the man who wore them. The crew is standing around, but nobody's there.

And then they all look at you. Not because you're smarter. Not because you're stronger. But because you're the one with the title, the clipboard, the key to the trailer. And everybody knows what that means: you're the one who has to call.

I've heard men say that the phone looked like it was glowing on the desk, like it was daring them to touch it. One foreman told me he couldn't even look at it — he just paced, muttering half-sentences under his breath, trying to practice something that would never come out right. Another told me he sat with it in his hand for twenty minutes, staring, because once you dial, there's no going back.

This is where responsibility gets real. Not the kind you sign at the bottom of a JHA. The kind that tears your gut out because you know the words you're about to say will wreck someone's world forever.

OSHA says you have eight hours to report a fatality. That's compliance. But there's no regulation for dialing a wife's number and listening to her answer. That's not compliance. That's hell.

Section 2 – The Ring and the Words

There are only a few sentences in this world that rip lives apart. One of them is:

"There's been an accident."

That's it. Three words. And you can't take them back once they're out.

You dial. One ring. Two. Three. And then — a voice. Sometimes it's the wife, already stressed from bills and kids. Sometimes it's a son just home from school. Sometimes it's a mother who trusted you to send her boy back safe. And in that moment, you're not a foreman. You're not a safety lead. You're the executioner's messenger.

Leaders who've done it describe the other end of the line. Screams that make your ears ring. Silence is so heavy it feels like the line went dead. Denial, anger, pleading — "No, not him. Please, no."

One man told me the hardest part wasn't the screaming. It was the sound of a child saying "Hello?" and realizing he was about to put a hole in that kid's life that would never close.

You can't sugarcoat it. You can't lie and say "He's going to be fine" when you already know the ambulance went the other way. Every word you speak cuts into somebody's soul, and you carry the echo of their reaction with you forever.

Psychologists call it secondary trauma

Mental_Physiological_Toll_Blog

. They say it scars the brain almost as badly as living through the accident yourself. But in the trades, nobody gives you therapy. Nobody gives you time off. You hang up, and you carry it alone.

The Silence After Hanging Up

Here's the part nobody talks about what happens when you hang up.

The crew outside is still milling around, smoking, whispering. The company wants a report. Maybe the sheriff's still on site. But you're sitting alone in that trailer, staring at a phone that feels like it's still ringing in your hand.

You can still hear the scream. You can still hear the silence. You can still hear the voice crack. And it doesn't stop. It plays repeatedly, long after the call ends.

Some guys go outside and bark orders, trying to bury it under anger. Some pour a cup of coffee they don't even drink. Some grab a bottle that night and keep drinking until they can't remember the sound.

But it never really leaves. One old supervisor told me, "I still hear it thirty years later. I could tell you the pitch of her voice. I could tell you what time of day it was. I could tell you what the light looked like coming through the trailer blinds. That's how deep it cuts.

---

The Weight That Never Leaves

The call didn't end that day. It follows you.

I've met men who flinch every time their phone rings, even decades later. It doesn't matter if it's their daughter calling to check in. For one second, their stomach flips and they're back in that trailer.

This is survivor guilt in leadership. You weren't the one who got burned. You weren't the one who fell. But you were the one who said yes to the job, yes to the permit, yes to the schedule. And now you're the one who told the family their life is broken.

NIOSH has documented how leaders suffer after workplace fatalities: insomnia, drinking, depression, substance abuse

Mental_Physiological_Toll_Blog

. But numbers don't show the full picture. Numbers don't show a man lying awake at 2 a.m., staring at the ceiling, hearing the echo of that voice repeatedly.

One foreman told me he buried two men that day: the worker in the ground, and himself inside.

And here's the cruel part: nobody sees it. The company is moving on. The family grieves at home. The crew starts a new job. But the man who made the call carries that coffin inside him for the rest of his life.

---

## The Culture of Silence

And here's where it gets darker. Nobody talks about it. Not on the next job. Not at the safety meeting. The company might hand out a memo, maybe a quick "moment of silence," but then it's back to production.

Leaders who've made the call don't tell the young guys. They don't bring it up at lunch. They keep it locked down, because the trade has this unspoken rule: don't show weakness. Don't admit what it did to you.

So, the ghosts pile up. Every foreman who's ever made that call walks around with them. You can see it in their eyes if you look closely — the thousand-yard stare, the way they tighten their jaw when the phone rings. But they won't say a word.

This silence is poison. It eats leaders alive. And worse, it keeps the lesson from being passed down. Apprentices don't know how heavy the phone is, so they don't fear it. And without that fear, shortcuts creep back in.

---

The Leadership Survival Standard

Here's the raw truth: when you allow shortcuts, when you rush a job, when you look the other way — you're not just risking someone's life. You're risking being the one who has to dial their home and listen to their world collapse.

That's what safety theater won't show you. Zero-incident banners don't prepare you for this. Production schedules don't shield you from it. The only thing that keeps you safe from that phone is discipline.

NFPA 70E makes it clear: leaders are responsible for ensuring safe practices

Mental_Physiological_Toll_Blog

. OSHA holds supervisors accountable for lockouts, training, and controls. But here's the thing: fines aren't the worst punishment. Courtrooms aren't the worst punishment.

The worst punishment is sitting in a trailer with a phone burning in your hand, knowing you're about to wreck a family with three words.

That's the leadership survival standard: don't let your name, your choices, or your silence be the reason you ever must make that call.

Turning the Phone Into a Shield

So how do you keep yourself from that moment? You treat survival like your life — and your crew's lives — depend on it. Because they do.

Fix hazards immediately. Don't wait for paperwork. Don't wait for the next shift. Fix it now.

Train for real. Don't pencil-whip signoffs. Don't hand a meter to a kid who's not ready.

Make permits sacred. An energized work permit isn't ink. It's blood. Your signature is your conscience.

Break the silence. Reward crews for speaking up. Build trust so they don't hide hazards. Every hidden hazard is a future phone call.

This is what it means to turn the phone into a shield. It's making sure it never rings for you.


Epilogue – Don't Be the One

Survival in the trades isn't just about walking out yourself. It's about not being the one who destroys someone else's life with your voice.

Here's the dark truth: when a worker dies, the family buries a son, a daughter, a father, a mother. But the leader who makes that call buries himself alive. He carries it every day, in silence.

So, before you let something slide, before you shrug off a lockout, before you say "just get it done," ask yourself:

If this goes wrong, am I ready to make that call?

Because if the answer is no, then you already know what to do.

Don't be the one.

Chapter 16

Carrying Ghosts

## Chapter 16

### The Ones Who Never Left

Every crew has ghosts.
Not Hollywood shadows. Not campfire stories. Real ghosts — the men and women who didn't make it out of the gate. The ones whose names still hang in the breakroom air or get mumbled at a bar years later.

You don't see their faces every day, but you feel them. You walk past lockers still locked, padlocks rusting around boots that will never walk again. You pick up a drill and see another man's initials carved into the plastic. You drive on the same road he drove on his last morning.

The worst part isn't the accident itself. It's the morning after. The crew shows up, heads down. The boss clears his throat and says a few stiff words. Then everyone tries to act normally, but nothing is normal. The first joke falls flat. The first laugh sounds forced. Every man feels the empty space, but nobody wants to say it out loud.

Some folks think time buries ghosts. It doesn't. They don't stay behind. They follow you. Into the next job. Into your truck. Into your sleep.

The only choice is how you carry them. Wrong, and they poison you. Right, and they make sure no one else joins them.

### Where Ghosts Live on the Jobsite

Ghosts don't hide in the shadows. They live in the things you walk past every day.

The locker that never opens. A lock with dust on it. A nameplate with tape peeling. The faint smell of leather and sweat inside. New hires ask, *"Whose locker is that?"* and the room goes quiet.

The lunchbox that never moves. It still has a spoon inside, maybe a faded sticker. Nobody has the heart to throw it out. Nobody dares touch it either.

The tool on the bench. A pair of lineman's pliers with tape wrapped just the way he liked. You reach for them out of habit — and stop.

The corner of the site where voices drop. A scaffold where a man fell. A panel where the blast took him. The crew gets louder walking toward it, then quiet when they pass.

The paperwork. Root cause reports. OSHA logs. Bullet points typed in clean language. But no report ever captures the scream, the smell of burnt insulation, or the sound of a body hitting concrete.

The half-finished story. Someone starts telling a memory, almost says the name, and swallows it. That silence is heavier than words.

Ghosts live in the open. If you think the site forgets, you haven't been paying attention.

The Weight They Put on the Living

Carrying ghosts isn't light. It sits on your chest, even if you never admit it.

It shows up in ways you don't expect. Breaker trips and the pop makes your stomach drop. You pull up to a scaffold and your palms sweat even though the ties are right. You second-guess every label because you know one lied.

I've seen men keep a burnt glove in their bag, a reminder to zip up every time. I've seen men who refuse to turn their back on a panel ever again. And I've seen men drink until names stop echoing in their heads.

Survivor guilt is real. *Why him, not me?* That question is a weight men carry in silence. NIOSH calls it secondary trauma 【NIOSH, 2018】 — the scars left on survivors. Crews just call it *"deal with it."* But "deal with it" usually means bury it under alcohol, anger, or silence.

And silence doesn't heal it. Silence rots.

## How Crews Hide Their Ghosts

We're trained to be tough. Laugh it off. Push through. Hide the cracks. But ghosts leak through the cracks anyway.

Hiding shows up in three phrases:

*"Accidents happen."*

*"It was just his time."*

*"We don't talk about that here."*

Every one of those phrases is a lie. Most "accidents" had a cause. It wasn't "his time." It was a suit not zipped, a breaker not tested, a tieoff skipped. And saying *"we don't talk about it"* doesn't protect anyone — it just guarantees another funeral.

I've worked sites where management's biggest concern wasn't fixing the hazard — it was *"controlling the message."* They thought silence would keep morale up. It didn't. It just told the crew: *Your friend is a statistic. Nothing changes.*

That's not respect. That's erasure. And erasing ghosts guarantees more of them.

## The Ghosts That Teach

But ghosts don't have to haunt. They can teach, if we let them.

Every scar has a lesson. Every fatality is a line in the sand. But only if we speak the truth out loud.

I've told apprentices straight: *"He trusted the tag. That's why you prove dead every time."* Or *"He took his gloves off because they felt clumsy. That's why you never do."*

That's not fearmongering. That's survival training.

The American Psychological Association calls it post-traumatic growth 【APA, 2020】—turning trauma into strength. In our trade, it means turning ghosts into discipline.

Because he didn't test, I always test.

Because he didn't zip, I always zip.

Because he didn't speak, I always speak.

The Ghosts We Take Home

The hardest ghosts don't stay on site. They ride home with you.

You walk through the door quietly. Your wife asks how your day was, and you say, *"Fine."* But it wasn't fine. You sit down at dinner, and the food has no taste. You stare at the TV but don't watch. Later, you lay in bed and replay it repeatedly — the scream, the flash, the silence.

Your wife notices the thousand-yard stare. Your kid notices you're quicker to snap. Maybe your daughter learns to stop asking questions because Dad's too tired. Maybe your son thinks anger is normal because he sees it more than laughter.

That's how ghosts poison homes. Not because families see them, but because they live through you.

The construction industry has one of the highest suicide rates of any profession CDC, 2020. That's not random. That's ghosts carried wrong. Men drink to quiet them. They isolate. They broke up marriages. And sometimes they decide it's easier to leave than to carry the weight another day.

But ghosts don't have to rot your family. If you tell the story on your terms — with your brothers in the trade, with your crew, maybe with someone trained to listen — you stop the ghost from owning you.

Talking about it isn't weakness. It's survival.

## Honoring Ghosts Instead of Hiding Them

The only right way to carry ghosts is to honor them. Not with silence. Not with shame. With respect.

That means:

Tell their stories. Don't sanitize it. Don't hide the cause. "He didn't test." "He skipped the tie-off." Those words sting, but they save.

Change the culture. If someone died from a shortcut, that shortcut dies with him. Period.

Build rituals. Some crews leave a locker untouched. Some carve initials into steel. Some name rules after the fallen. That's not superstition — it's survival culture.

Speak their names. Pretending they never existed is worse than the accident itself.

Respect isn't silence. Respect is truth remembered.

---

## Carrying Them Without Breaking

There's a balance. You can't let ghosts drag you under. But you also can't block them out. The balance is carrying them in a way that changes how you work, not how you live.

That means ghosts should sharpen your discipline. They should echo in toolbox talks, in training, in habits. But they don't belong at the dinner table.

That's the difference between carrying with pride and carrying with shame. Pride says, *"His loss keeps me sharp."* Shame says, *"His loss is my fault."* One keeps you alive. The other eats you alive.

Ghosts don't leave. But they don't have to break you either.

Epilogue — The Crew That Walks with You

We don't work alone. We never have. Every time you walk onto a site, you walk with your crew — the living, and the dead.

The living depends on you to call stop, to hold the line, to demand discipline. Dead depend on you to tell their stories, to carry their lessons, to make sure their deaths weren't wasted.

That's what survival really is. Not just walking out yourself but carrying ghosts the right way. Letting them sharpen you, not crush you.

So tomorrow, when you walk through the gate, look around. You're not alone. You're carrying ghosts. Make sure you carry them with respect. Make sure you carry them into a future where no more lockers stay locked, no more hard hats hang untouched, no more names get swallowed in silence.

Because ghosts don't leave. But you can make sure no more join them.

# Chapter 17

## Survival Isn't an Accident — It's a Legacy

Final Chapter

Introduction — Survival Isn't an Accident

If you've made it this far, you already know survival in the trades isn't luck. It's not a coin toss, and it's sure as hell not about being tougher than the next guy. It's deliberate. It's a series of choices — stacked, layered, reinforced — until they form a wall that protects you, your crew, and the people waiting for you at home.

This book was never about comfort. It's about survival. And survival isn't handed to you. It's earned — one decision at a time. Every glove worn, every test performed, every time you speak up instead of staying quiet — that's survival. And it's not just for you. It's for the guy next to you. It's for the family waiting at the gate.

According to the Bureau of Labor Statistics, electrical workers face one of the highest fatality rates in construction  That's not a statistic — that's a wake-up call. Survival isn't dramatic. It's not heroic. It's disciplined. It's boring sometimes. But it's the only way to make it home.

And here's the truth: survival isn't just physical. It's mental. It's emotional. It's spiritual. It's the ability to walk away from a job site knowing you didn't compromise your values, your safety, or your crew. That kind of survival builds something bigger than a paycheck — it builds legacy.


What It Means to Be Grounded

Electricians understand grounding better than most. Without it, current doesn't stop — it hunts. It searches for flesh, for steel, for a path home. And when it finds you, it doesn't forgive.

But grounding isn't just about wire. It's about people. A man without grounding drifts. Pride pulls him one way, pressure another. Eventually, he crosses lines he never meant to cross.

I've seen ungrounded men. They swagger. They cut corners. They mock the rules. They think nothing can touch them — until the day it does. Hospital beds are full of them. Cemeteries too.

To be grounded in this trade means being tied into something solid: discipline, respect, brotherhood, legacy. It means knowing your limits. Respecting the hazard. Refusing to gamble with someone else's life just to look fast or tough.

Grounding keeps you steady when chaos hits. It anchors you when everything else is rushing forward. It ensures that when the shift ends, you walk out the gate alive.

The National Fire Protection Association (NFPA 70E) defines grounding as a critical safeguard against electrical shock and arc flash

. But the deeper truth is this: grounding is a mindset. It's the difference between surviving and becoming a statistic. And grounding isn't just personal — it's cultural. A grounded crew doesn't panic. They don't freeze when the unexpected hits. They fall back on training, on trust, on the code they've built together. That's the kind of crew that survives.

Grounding also means humility. It means knowing that no matter how many years you've been in the trade, the hazard doesn't care. It doesn't care about your certifications, your reputation, or your ego. It only cares about physics — and physics doesn't forgive.

The Contractor's Code

Every crew has a code — even if it's not written down. The question is whether it's worth following.

Here's mine:

Show up prepared. No excuses. No "I forgot my gloves." No hangovers on the job.

Respect the hazard. Every wire, every scaffold, every confined space. Assume it can kill you. Because it can.

Protect your crew. Never send a rookie where you wouldn't go first.

Speak the truth. If it's unsafe, call it. Even if it costs you popularity or pay.

Finish with honor. Every job ends, but your reputation doesn't.

A code is only real if it costs something. Second you bend it for convenience, it's no code at all. Write yours. Live it. Make sure your crew sees it in action. Because when your words fade, your code remains.

I've seen a crew fall apart because the code was just talk. And I've seen crews survive the worst because the code was lived. OSHA doesn't regulate integrity — but it's the backbone of every safe job site

And here's the truth: your code is contagious. If you cut corners, your crew will too. If you hold the line, they'll follow. That's how culture is built — not by rules, but by example.

A real code doesn't just protect you — it protects the guy who's still learning. It protects the one who's afraid to speak up. It protects the one who doesn't know yet that shortcuts kill. That's why your code matters. It's not just about you. It's about everyone who watches you work.

Leadership That Lasts

Leadership isn't about titles or stripes. It's about what you do when nobody else wants to step up. Bad leaders bury crews. They worship numbers. They punish anyone who slows down for safety. They cover up accidents to protect their own careers. Their legacy is silence, bitterness, and ghosts.

Good leaders save lives. They stand firm when the pressure comes crushing. They take the heat from management, so their crew doesn't have to. They give rookies space to learn without fear. They make the unpopular call when it's the right one.

If you're responsible for even one other person, you're a leader. Every choice you make teaches someone else how to act. If you gamble, they'll gamble. If you cut corners, so will they. Ask yourself: when the apprentice copies you, will you be proud of what they learned?

The Construction Industry Institute found that strong safety leadership directly correlates with lower incident rates and higher crew morale That's not theory — that's boots-on-the-ground reality.

Leadership isn't loud. It's consistent. It's the quiet voice that says, "We don't do it that way — not here." And leadership doesn't end when the shift does. It follows you home. It shows up in how you talk about the job, how you treat your family, how you carry the weight of responsibility. The best leaders don't just build projects — they build people.

Leadership also means accountability. It means owning your mistakes. It means showing your crew that safety isn't weakness — it's strength. It's the kind of strength that keeps fathers alive, keeps mothers from burying their sons, keeps legacies intact.

The Next Generation

This is where it gets personal. Because this book isn't just about us — it's about them. The ones coming behind us. The apprentices. The rookies. The kids who don't know yet what they don't know.

They're not learning survival from manuals. They're learning it from us. They memorize what we do — not what we say.

When you clip in every time, they notice. When you test before you touch, they see it. When you call stop even though it costs you time, they remember. And when you shrug at a shortcut, when you gamble, when you laugh off PPE — they remember that too.

I once had a kid shadow me, nervous and green. At lunch, he asked, "How do you know when it's too dangerous?" I told him, "If your gut says stop, stop. I'll back you up." That moment mattered more than any tool I showed him that week. Years later, he told me he remembered that sentence when he walked away from a job that didn't feel right. That's survival culture.

The next generation will inherit whatever we hand them. If we hand them silence, they'll inherit shortcuts. If we hand them stories honestly about near misses and scars — they'll inherit caution. If we hand them standards, they'll inherit discipline.

The National Safety Council reports that younger workers are disproportionately injured on the job due to lack of training and mentorship That's not their fault. That's ours.

And it's not just about jobsites. It's about classrooms, trade schools, and orientation programs. It's about whether we're willing to tell the hard stories — the ones that hurt, the ones that teach. Because if we don't, someone else will. And they might not tell it right.

The future of this trade depends on what we hand down. Every choice we make is shaping a culture that either carries more ghosts — or fewer.

And let's be honest — the next generation is watching everything. They're watching how we treat each other. How we handle pressure. How we respond to mistakes. If we want them to inherit a culture of survival, we have to live it out loud.

Legacy Reflections

Legacy is the heaviest word in this book. It's not a plaque on a wall or a certificate in a frame. Legacy is what people say when your name comes up after you're gone.

On the jobsite, legacy sounds like this:

"He always tested."

"He never let you cut corners."

Or "Don't do it like him — that's how he got killed."

At home, legacy is even heavier. It's the chair that stays filled or the chair that stays empty. It's whether your kids grow up with a father or with stories. It's whether your wife gets gray hairs laughing with you — or folds a flag while the crew lowers their heads.

I've stood in both places. I've seen crews whisper about men who didn't make it, and I've seen kids run to their dads at the gate. There's no comparison. One leaves silence. The other leaves life.

Legacy is written one choice at a time. A shortcut can stain it forever. The habit of discipline can strengthen it for generations.

Your legacy isn't about how many hours you billed or how many jobs you have closed. It's about whether your name is tied to shortcuts or to standards. Whether your crew trusted you or feared you. Whether your family remembers you in life — or grieves you in silence.

Legacy isn't built in the spotlight. It's built in the quiet moments — when you choose caution over speed, truth over comfort, safety over pride.

And legacy isn't just what you leave behind — it's what you build while you're here. Every time you choose safety, you're building a legacy of life. Every time you speak up, you're building a legacy of courage. Every time you mentor someone, you're building a legacy of survival.

Final Thoughts — Make It Home

At the end of everything, this whole book boils down to one truth: make it home.

Not half-alive. Not with scars that make your kids stare. Not with excuses in your pocket. Whole. Alive. Present.

Every shortcut gambles with that. Every excuse risks it. Every act of discipline protects it.

I don't care if you've been in this trade for two months or two decades. The hazard doesn't care either. Electricity doesn't play favorites. Falls don't check résumés. The ground doesn't care about pride.

Make it home. For your crew. For your family. For yourself.

This isn't just a job. It's a life. And the measure of that life isn't how fast you worked or how many jobs you finished. It's whether the people you love see you walk through the door at the end of the day.

So, draw your line. Hold it. Protect it. And never forget survival isn't dramatic. It isn't luck. It's deliberate. It's disciplined. And it's worth everything.

bonus

## The Contractor's Survival Creed

I will show up prepared.
I will respect the hazard.
I will test before I touch.
I will zip before I step.
I will lock before I trust.
I will clip in, even for one step.
I will protect my crew as if they are family.
I will speak the truth, even when it costs me.
I will not gamble with shortcuts.
I will honor those who didn't make it home.
I will carry their lessons forward. I
will make it home.

*This is not a slogan. It's survival. And I will live it.*

---

## Job Briefing Survival Checklist

Did we identify every source of energy?

Did we test before touching — every circuit, every time?

Did every crew member hear the briefing, or did someone get left out?

Do we have the right PPE for the job, not just what's convenient?

Who has the authority to call stop? (Answer: Everyone)

## Daily Grounding Reminders

Am I rested, sober, and focused?

Do I have the right tools, and are they in serviceable condition?

Do I know where my escape path is if things go wrong?

Am I carrying discipline, or gambling with shortcuts?

Will I walk out the gate the same way I walked in?

The Crew Safety Code (Field Version)

Protect yourself.

Protect your partner.

Protect your legacy.

---

Letter to the Next Generation

To the ones coming up behind us — listen close.

You don't know yet what you don't know. That's not an insult, it's the truth. Every one of us started there. Wide-eyed. Green. Hungry to prove ourselves. I see it in you — the pride, the swagger, the willingness to go first. But hear me: pride doesn't make you invincible. Hazard doesn't care how strong you are.

Every scar on my hands is a lesson I paid for. Some of my brothers paid with more than scars. And I'm telling you straight — if you don't respect this trade, it will take from you. It will take fast, and it won't give back.

So, here's what I want you to know:

Slow down. Nothing you build is worth more than your life.

Test every time. Don't trust a label or another man's word.

Speak up. If it feels wrong, call stop. I'll back you up. Any real leader will.

Learn from ghosts. Ask about the names crews don't like to say. Their stories will save you.

You are the next generation of this trade. You will carry the culture we leave behind. If we hand you shortcuts, you'll inherit funerals. If we hand you discipline, you'll inherit survival.

Someday, you'll be the one apprentices looking to for answers. What will you hand them? A shrug, or a standard?

Carry discipline. Carry respect. Carry the creed. And above all else — make it home.

Because the greatest thing you can give this trade isn't how fast you worked or how much you produced. The greatest thing you can give

is your example, your survival, and the proof that it's possible to build a career, a legacy, and a life without becoming another ghost.

Stay grounded. Stay alive. Carry the line forward.

— Bobby Duncan

## Works Cited

### References

American Psychological Association. (2020). *Trauma and posttraumatic growth.* APA.org.

American Psychological Association. (2020). *Trauma and stress effects on the body.* APA.org.

ANSI/ISEA. (n.d.). ANSI/ISEA 105—*Hand protection classification and testing.*

ANSI/ISEA. (n.d.). ANSI/ISEA Z87.1—*Eye and face protection devices.*

ASTM International. (n.d.). ASTM F496—*Standard specification for in-service care of insulating gloves and sleeves.*

ASTM International. (n.d.). ASTM F1506—*Standard performance specification for flame resistant and electric arc rated protective clothing.*

ASTM International. (n.d.). ASTM F2178—*Standard test method for determining the arc rating of face protective products.*

ASTM International. (n.d.). ASTM F1505—*Standard specification for insulated and insulating hand tools.*

Bureau of Labor Statistics. (2023). *Fatal occupational injuries report.* U.S. Department of Labor.

Centers for Disease Control and Prevention. (2020). *Suicide rates by industry and occupation.*

Edison, T. A. (1932). Quoted in *Harper's Monthly.*

Electrical Safety Foundation International. (n.d.). *Electrical injury and fatality data reports.*

European Union. (2016). *Regulation (EU) 2016/425—Conformity assessment and PPE categories.*

Franklin, B. (1733). *Poor Richard's Almanack.*

Institute of Electrical and Electronics Engineers. (2018). *IEEE 1584—Guide for performing arc flash hazard calculations.* IEEE Standards Association.

International Electrotechnical Commission. (n.d.). *IEC 61482-2—Live working—Protective clothing against the thermal hazards of an electric arc.*

International Organization for Standardization. (n.d.). *ISO 45001—Occupational health and safety management systems—Requirements with guidance for use.*

National Fire Protection Association. (2023). *NFPA 70: National Electrical Code (NEC).* 2023 ed.

National Fire Protection Association. (2024). *NFPA 70E: Standard for electrical safety in the workplace.* 2024 ed.

National Institute for Occupational Safety and Health. (2015). *Hierarchy of controls and incident case studies.*

National Institute for Occupational Safety and Health. (2018). *Stress at work.* Centers for Disease Control and Prevention.

National Institute for Occupational Safety and Health. (n.d.). *Fatality assessment and control evaluation (FACE) reports.*

Occupational Safety and Health Administration. (2024). *29 CFR 1904—Recording and reporting occupational injuries and illness.* U.S. Department of Labor.

Occupational Safety and Health Administration. (2024). *29 CFR 1910.132—Personal protective equipment; general requirements and employer duties.* U.S. Department of Labor.

Occupational Safety and Health Administration. (2024). 29 CFR 1910.147—*The control of hazardous energy (lockout/tagout)*. U.S. Department of Labor.

Occupational Safety and Health Administration. (2024). 29 CFR 1910.269(c)—*Job briefing*. U.S. Department of Labor.

Occupational Safety and Health Administration. (2024). 29 CFR 1910.332—*Training*. U.S. Department of Labor.

Occupational Safety and Health Administration. (2024). 29 CFR 1910.333—*Selection and use of work practices*. U.S. Department of Labor.

U.S. Navy. (n.d.). *Operational risk management (ORM) principles*. Naval Education and Training Command.

www.ingramcontent.com/pod-product-compliance
Lightning Source LLC
Chambersburg PA
CBHW020543030426

42337CB00013B/958